HOUSING MARKET IMPACTS OF RENT CONTROL

The Washington, D.C. Experience

URBAN INSTITUTE REPORT 90–1

Margery A. Turner

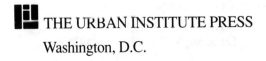 THE URBAN INSTITUTE PRESS
Washington, D.C.

363.5
T94 ho

THE URBAN INSTITUTE PRESS
2100 M Street, N.W.
Washington, D.C. 20037

Library of Congress Cataloging in Publication Data

Housing Market Impacts of Rent Control: the Washington, D.C. experience / Margery A. Turner

1. Rent Control--Washington (D.C.) 2. Rental Housing--Washington (D.C.) I. Title. II Series.

HD7288.85.U62W188   1990   89-25002
                                                                              CIP

(Urban Institute Reports; 90-1, ISSN 0897-7399)

ISBN 0-87766-443-9
ISBN 0-87766-442-0 (casebound)

Printed in the United States of America.

Distributed by University Press of America

4720 Boston Way   3 Henrietta Street
Lanham, MD 20706   London WC2E 8LU ENGLAND

URBAN INSTITUTE REPORTS

are designed to provide rapid dissemination of research and policy findings. Each report contains timely information and is rigorously reviewed to uphold the highest standards of policy research and analysis.

The Urban Institute is a nonprofit policy research and educational organization established in Washington, D.C., in 1968. Its staff investigates the social and economic problems confronting the nation and government policies and programs designed to alleviate such problems. The Institute disseminates significant findings of its research through the publications program of its Press. The Institute has two goals for work in each of its research areas: to help shape thinking about societal problems and efforts to solve them, and to improve government decisions and performance by providing better information and analytic tools.

Through work that ranges from broad conceptual studies to administrative and technical assistance, Institute researchers contribute to the stock of knowledge available to public officials and private individuals and groups concerned with formulating and implementing more efficient and effective government policy.

Conclusions or opinions expressed in Institute publications are those of the authors and do not necessarily reflect the views of other staff members, officers or trustees of the Institute, advisory groups, or any organizations that provide financial support to the Institute.

ACKNOWLEDGMENTS

This report is based on a study funded by the District of Columbia's Department of Consumer and Regulatory Affairs. Its successful completion would not have been possible without the help of many individuals who contributed information, guidance, and opinions throughout the course of the study.

The firm of Lawrence Johnson and Associates collected and coded data from D.C. tenants and landlords. The Mayor's Tenant-Provider Advisory Committee participated in questionnaire development and provided advice on data collection and analysis. Staff members of the Department of Consumer and Regulatory Affairs, particularly Valerie Lemmie, Jacqueline Davison, and Howard Lewis made invaluable contributions of information, time, and expertise.

Urban Institute staff members who participated in data collection and analysis include G. Thomas Kingsley, Marcia Carroll, Amina H.N. Elmi, Kathleen G. Heintz, Barbara Lipman, Martha Nicholson, Douglas B. Page, Makiko Ueno, and J. Christopher Walker. Finally, Raymond J. Struyk, Lee Bawden, and James C. Turner all helped by providing critical commentary on earlier drafts of this report.

CONTENTS

Figures

ABSTRACT

Affordability is the most serious housing problem confronting renter households. Rent control offers the promise of making housing more affordable at no public cost. But it also runs the risk of eliminating profitability and leading to deterioration in the rental housing stock.

The D.C. rent control system , set up in 1975, does not fix rent levels but controls the frequency and amount of rent increases. It is a moderate scheme that explicitly seeks to maintain the profitability of rental housing investments.

Findings indicate that D.C. rents have been controlled (although not altogether equitably), and that rent control has not eliminated profitability. This suggests that the rental housing market may have imperfections that make rent control a legitimate public sector intervention: imperfect information, high transaction costs, a segmented market, high entry costs, and barriers to entry.

Affordability has become the most serious housing problem confronting renter households. With the shrinking federal resources allocated to housing assistance, and the less than full replacement of lost federal funds by state programs, local governments are under increasing pressure to make rental housing more affordable. Rent control offers the promise of making housing more affordable at virtually no cost to the public sector. But it also runs the risk of restricting profits to such an extent that the housing stock deteriorates.

The D.C. Rent Control System

The D.C. rent control system was established in 1975. About two-thirds of the rental stock is subject to controls, with the following categories exempt: small units, new and substantially renovated units, units in continuously vacant buildings, co-op units, and subsidized units. Even the controlled units do not have fixed rent levels. A complex system regulates both the frequency and amount of rent increases. Properly licensed and registered units can increase rents annually by the Consumer Price Index. When a unit is vacated, its rent can be increased by 12 percent or up to the rent ceiling, whichever is higher. Landlords can petition to increase rent ceilings to reflect certain cost increases. And landlords can negotiate voluntary agreements with tenants to increase rents.

Data

The report is based on an extensive database, including new data collected from seven major sources: telephone interviews with 3,000 D.C. renters and 600 renters in surrounding suburbs, financial statements for 814 controlled rental properties, questionnaires completed by owners and managers of 244 controlled rental properties, inventory of all additions to and losses from the D.C. rental stock between May 1985 and April 1987, one year's history of housing code enforcement activity for controlled rental properties, volume and case-by-case disposition of housing provider and tenant petitions, and application and participation data for the District's Tenant Assistance Program. In addition, data on households and housing conditions were extracted from the American Housing Survey.

Findings

D.C. rent control has kept rents lower than they would have been in its absence. The monthly rent for the average unit would be at least $50 higher and possibly $200 higher without rent control.

These benefits are not spread equitably or efficiently. By targeting benefits to long-term stayers, D.C. rent control provides greatest benefits to lower income renters, elderly households, and families with children. But affluent renters also obtain direct benefits if they stay in a unit for an extended period. And poor renters, if they move, pay rents just as high as those that would prevail on the open market.

Rent control has not eliminated profitability. After accounting for appreciation gains and tax benefits, investment in D.C. rental housing today compares favorably with alternative investment opportunities.

Whether rent control is responsible for housing deficiencies in the District's rental stock is unclear. About one in five rental units is physically deficient. Without controls, gross rent revenues would have been 33 percent higher. Landlords say they would have used the increase for better maintenance. But even with rent control the proportion of units that are physically deficient in the District has declined from a total share of 26 percent to one of 20 percent, and the rate of deficiencies is *higher* among the *exempt* units.

The size of the rental stock declined precipitously during the period of rent control in the District, but many cities without rent control have witnessed similar declines. The relative attractiveness of home ownership, expansion of suburban housing opportunities for minorities, and the basic costs of rental housing production appear to the critical determinants of the number of units added and lost to the rental housing stock. This conclusion is supported by the fact that the supply of rental housing in the District has begun to respond to renewed demand pressures.

Despite this supply response, the District faces a persistent shortage of units that low- and moderate-income households can afford. A substantial share of the units added to the rental stock in recent years were developed as condominiums and could easily be converted to owner-occupancy if demand swings back in that direction.

The units at greatest risk of being removed from the stock are those with very low rents and chronic code violations. These qualify for hardship rent increases, but applications have not been filed. Presumably the administrative and financial burden of applying for them has been the primary hurdle. Tenants are simply too poor to pay the rent levels necessary to make the buildings profitable. A full solution to the District's shortage of affordable housing would require a combination of direct subsidies to poor households, systematic efforts to preserve the properties currently occupied by low- and moderate-income renters, and production of additional units set aside for needy households.

Conclusions

Economic theory suggests that, over the long run, any substantial price effect (reduced rents) must yield a supply effect (lower quality/fewer units). Yet this evidence suggests that D.C. rent control has had little or no supply effect despite a decade of moderated rent increases. How can these results be explained in the context of a reasonably competitive market for rental housing?

First, like other rent control programs implemented in U.S cities in the 1970s--and unlike those implemented earlier--the District's system provides incentives for landlords to maintain their existing rental properties and to produce new ones. It is a moderate scheme that explicitly seeks to maintain the profitability of investment in rental housing.

But if the program has in fact moderated rents by at least $50 a month, in the absence of rent control D.C. landlords would have earned excessive profits over an extended period--as did indeed happen in other markets. This is inconsistent with economic theory, unless there are imperfections in the rental housing market that permit excess profits in the longer run. Our study suggests that there are indeed imperfections that make rent control a legitimate public sector intervention. These include: imperfect information, high transaction costs, a segmented market, high entry costs, and barriers to entry.

Chapter One

RENT CONTROL IN U.S. CITIES

Rent control is one of the most persistent and hotly debated of all housing policy issues. In the years ahead, the pros and cons of rent regulation will continue to receive attention from state and local governments, as they attempt to grapple with escalating rent burdens. Between 1975 and 1988, real rent levels increased by 17 percent, while real incomes among renter households actually fell by about 4 percent. High interest rates and operating costs, "gentrification," and condominium conversions all contributed in varying degrees to rapid increases in rent levels, with the result that, today, over two-thirds (69.9 percent) of all poor renters spend more than half of their income on housing.[1] Clearly, affordability has become the most serious housing problem confronting renter households.

Federal housing assistance programs have not been sufficient to close the growing affordability gap. During the 1980s, the federal government slashed the level of resources allocated to housing assistance, virtually eliminating programs that subsidized the construction of low-cost apartment projects. The number of additional households receiving federal housing help plummeted from a high of over 300,000 annually in the mid-1970s to less than 100,000 by the mid-1980s.[2] Many state governments have stepped into the vacuum left by the federal government, but have not been able to replace the level of federal funding that has been withdrawn. Thus, local governments are under increasing pressure to make rental housing more affordable--or, at a minimum, to slow the pace at which rents are rising.

Rent control offers the tantalizing promise of making housing more affordable at virtually no cost to the public sector. However, by restricting rent levels, rent control may also restrict profits so severely that landlords neither maintain their existing properties nor build new ones. If so, local efforts to moderate housing costs may actually do more harm than good. Public debate over the relative costs and benefits of rent control has resulted in two distinct "generations" of local rent control in the United States.

Wartime shortages of housing units and building materials led to the imposition of a "first generation" of stringent rent controls in several communities during World War I, and nationally, as part of a federal program of wage and price controls, during World War II. By the early 1950s, however, New York was the only state in which local governments were authorized to regulate rents. Many analysts have cited the problems of New York City's rental housing market as evidence that rent controls do more harm than good. Nevertheless, the rapid inflation of the 1970s resulted in a "second generation" of rent control programs, with four more states--New Jersey, Connecticut, California, and Massachusetts as well as the District of Columbia-- authorizing localities to implement controls. Today, rent controls are in effect in over 200 U.S. communities.

Virtually all of these "second generation" rent control programs moderate the rate of rent inflation rather than holding rents fixed, and most provide explicit incentives for new construction and renovations to the existing stock of rental housing. More specifically, almost all U.S. rent control programs today permit rents to increase each year by some percentage that is intended to reflect the rate of increases in operating costs. In addition, many ordinances allow for larger rent increases when units are vacated, with some communities allowing rent levels to rise to market levels upon turnover. Under most second generation programs, newly constructed apartment buildings are exempt from controls, and landlords can "pass through" the costs of building improvements in the form of higher rents. Finally, virtually all of the rent control programs in effect today contain "hardship" provisions, allowing landlords to petition for relief in cases of extraordinary cost increases or unacceptably low rates of return.

The District of Columbia established its current system of rent stabilization in 1975. The bulk (approximately two-thirds) of the District's rental stock is subject to controls, but five important categories of rental units are exempt: (1) units owned by small landlords (individuals with fewer than five D.C. rental units in all); (2) new and substantially renovated units (those added to the stock after 1975); (3) units in vacant buildings (if the buildings were continuously vacant since 1985); (4) co-op units; and (5) subsidized units (except those subsidized through the local housing allowance program).

Under the District's program, rent levels are not held fixed. Instead, both the frequency and amount of rent increases are regulated. For units that are properly licensed and registered and that comply with the city's housing code, rents can increase annually by the previous year's consumer price index (CPI). And when a unit is vacated, its rent can be increased by 12 percent or up to the rent ceiling for a comparable unit in the same property, whichever is higher. In addition, landlords can petition to increase rent ceilings to reflect the cost increases associated with capital improvements, substantial rehabilitation, or changes in services and facilities. For properties in financial hardship, rent increases can be approved to generate a 12 percent cash return on equity. And, finally, landlords can negotiate voluntary agreements with their tenants to increase rent ceilings.

The complexity of these exemption and rent adjustment provisions reflects the District's effort to balance the goal of reducing housing costs for the city's renters against the need to ensure that rental housing is sufficiently profitable to attract investment so that the supply of good quality rental units is sustained.

This report presents the results of a comprehensive study by The Urban Institute of the impact of rent control on the availability, adequacy, and affordability of rental housing in Washington, D.C. The study was mandated by the District's City Council in 1985, when it voted to extend the existing system of controls for another five years.[3] Although numerous theoretical and empirical analyses of rent control have been conducted in the United States, none has adequately addressed the City Council's specific concerns about the moderate system of controls implemented in the District of Columbia.[4]

The analysis described here was designed to empirically test a set of explicit hypotheses about how rent control affects the local housing market. Figure 1.1 depicts the full range of possible market impacts that might be expected to result from the regulation of rent levels. The most obvious and direct effect of rent control is on rents--with the assumption being that controls will reduce rents for at least some segments of the inventory. To the extent that rent control has any significant impact on prevailing rent levels, it may also have other effects, on both the supply and demand sides of the rental housing market. On the demand side:

- Changes in rent levels may make housing more or less affordable for some households and may, therefore, alter local mobility rates--including both voluntary and involuntary mobility.

FIGURE 1.1 POSSIBLE IMPACTS OF RENT CONTROL ON MARKET DYNAMICS

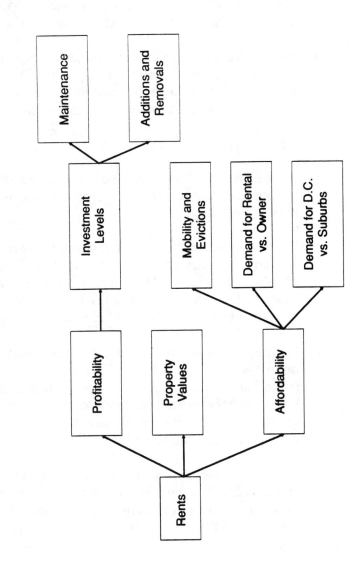

- A change in District rents may alter the relative costs of owning versus renting enough to change the tenure choices of some District households.

- Similarly, a change in District rent levels may alter the relative costs of rental housing in the District and the surrounding suburbs enough to change the location choices of some renter households.

And on the supply side of the market:

- If rents are significantly affected by controls, then property values and property appreciation may also be affected.

- Rents, values, and expected appreciation are all key components of the profitability of rental housing investment. Thus, if rent controls affect these factors, they will alter the profitability of investment in the District's rental housing sector.

- Profitability is a primary determinant of investment levels. Therefore, to the extent that rent control alters the profitability of rental real estate, it may alter the amount of maintenance and capital improvements performed for existing properties, thereby affecting the adequacy of the stock.

- Changes in profitability may also alter the volume of units added to the rental housing stock as well as the number of units removed from the stock, thereby affecting the availability of rental units in the District.

To address these hypotheses comprehensively, The Urban Institute assembled an extensive database, including new data collected from seven major sources:

- telephone interviews with 3,000 D.C. renters and 600 renters in surrounding suburban jurisdictions, covering household characteristics, housing conditions, rent levels, and attitudes toward the rent control program;

- financial statements for 814 controlled rental properties collected from D.C. administrative files;

- questionnaires completed by owners or managers of 244 controlled rental properties, covering their experience with and attitudes toward rent control in the District;

- inventory of all additions to and losses from the District's rental housing stock between May 1985 and April 1987;

- one year's history of housing code enforcement activity for controlled rental properties;

- volume and case-by-case disposition of housing provider and tenant petitions;

- application and participation data for the District's Tenant Assistance Program.

In addition, data on households and housing conditions were extracted from the American Housing Survey (AHS) for the Washington area and for other metropolitan areas in the U.S.

SUMMARY OF FINDINGS

The most severe and widespread problem confronting renters in the District of Columbia is a shortage of units that are affordable for households with low and moderate incomes. Rent control is neither the cause nor the complete solution for this problem. The existing system of controls achieves its objective of reducing rents for the majority of D.C. units, but it has by no means eliminated the problem of excessive housing cost burdens. And although there is legitimate cause for concern that an excessively restrictive policy of rent control might ultimately limit the supply of rental housing, the empirical evidence does not indicate that the city's rent control program has had a significant adverse impact on housing supply. In fact, the quality of the District's housing stock is better today than in 1974, and changes in the overall size of the rental inventory appear to be much more sensitive to nationwide demographic and economic forces than to the local regulatory environment.

There is, of course, no way to observe empirically what D.C. rent levels would be in the absence of controls. For this analysis, market rents have been estimated based on patterns observed prior to the imposition of controls and on recent trends in uncontrolled central city housing markets. These estimates suggest that, in the absence of controls, the monthly rent for the average D.C. unit would be at least $50 higher than it is today, and possibly as much as $200 higher. Our best estimate is that today's rents average between $95 and $100 per month lower than they would be in the absence of controls, and that roughly three-quarters of D.C. renters would be paying higher rents in an unregulated market. According to these estimates, the District's existing system of controls has moderated increases in rent levels for most households, particularly for those who remain in their units for more than a year or two. By reducing prevailing rent levels, the system makes rental housing more affordable than it would be otherwise, with the result that the share of renters devoting more than 30 percent of their income toward housing is lower in D.C. than in other U.S. central cities.

However, not all D.C. renters benefit directly from controls. Because the city's rent control program allows larger rent increases when units change occupancy, the rent savings attributable to controls are greatest for households who remain in the same controlled units for more than a year or two. Recent movers generally appear to pay as much as they would in the absence of controls, since many landlords raise rents to the highest allowable levels at the time of turnover.

By targeting benefits to long-term stayers, rent control tends to provide the greatest rent savings to lower income renters, to elderly households, and to families with children. Affluent renters, as well as young singles and groups of young adults, also obtain direct benefits whenever they remain in controlled units for an extended number of years. And poor households who move are likely to pay rents that are just as high as those that would prevail in an uncontrolled market. Thus, not all the benefits of rent control are targeted equitably or efficiently.

During the 1980s the rate of rent increases generally kept pace with increases in operating costs, even for units that were continuously occupied. Although rent levels in the District today are lower on average than estimates suggest they would be in the absence of controls, the District's system of automatic rent adjustments appears to have compensated most landlords adequately for increases in operating costs. This may not have been true during the 1970s, when utility costs rose sharply and annual rent adjustments were limited to 10 percent even when the consumer price index was higher. During this period, the revenues of some landlords may have been eroded as a result of controls.

The majority of controlled units in the District generate relatively low cash returns. However, after accounting for appreciation gains and tax benefits, the profitability of investment in D.C. rental housing today compares favorably to alternative investment opportunities. In the absence of controls, the gross rent revenues would be higher, but the after-tax rate of return on investment would probably increase by only about two percentage points for small properties and by as much five percentage points for larger properties.

The evidence is mixed when it comes to determining whether rent control is responsible for housing deficiencies in the District's rental stock. A significant minority of D.C. rental units--about one in five--is physically deficient. On the one hand, the higher rent levels that we estimate would prevail in the absence of controls would increase landlords' gross rent revenues by an average of 33 percent. Many landlords indicate that they would use higher revenues to improve building maintenance or to address deferred maintenance problems; in fact, the increased revenue that would be realized in the absence of controls would probably be sufficient to improve maintenance substantially in at least half of the existing stock. On the other hand, however, the proportion of D.C. rental units that are physically deficient has actually declined since the implementation of rent control, from a total share of 26 percent to 20 percent, and the rate of deficiencies is higher among exempt units today than among units that are subject to controls.

Even in the absence of controls, the District's rental stock would have experienced a precipitous decline in size during the 1970s. The newly imposed system of local rent controls may have been a factor in the decisions of some landlords to remove properties from use or to convert them to owner-occupancy. However, since many uncontrolled central cities in the United States experienced the same pattern of decline, we conclude that widespread demographic and economic conditions were more important sources of the shrinkage in the District's rental inventory. Specifically, the relative attractiveness of homeownership, the expansion of suburban housing opportunities for minorities, and the basic costs of rental housing production appear to be the critical determinants of the number of units added to and lost from the District's rental housing stock.

In more recent years, the supply of rental housing in the District has begun to respond to renewed demand pressures, confirming that rent control is not the determining factor in investment decisionmaking. Starting in the early 1980s, demand for rental housing in the District began to stabilize, in part because rising interest rates, lower inflation, and reductions in marginal tax rates all contributed to make homeownership less affordable relative to rental housing. At first, the supply of rental units continued its decline, and the result was a dramatic drop in the rental vacancy rate, from 6.2 percent in 1981 to 2.5 percent in 1985. More recently, the District's rental stock has started to grow in size, increasing by about 1,600 units between 1985 and 1987. This turnaround represents a lagged market response to renewed levels of effective demand.

Despite the renewed level of rental housing production, the District faces a persistent shortage of units that low- and moderate-income households can afford. Today, fewer units are being removed from the inventory than in the 1970s and early 1980s, and more units are being added through substantial renovation and the conversion of nonresidential properties. However, these additions respond to a heightened level of demand from relatively affluent renters; most do not significantly expand the availability of affordable housing for poor and moderate-income renters in D.C. In fact, a substantial share of the units added to the rental stock in recent years were developed as condominiums and are being rented, rather than owner-occupied, for the time being. These units, which currently supplement the stock of rental housing, could easily be converted to owner-occupancy if demand pressures swing back in that direction.

The availability of low-cost rental housing is much more sensitive to the number of units lost from the stock each year than to the number of units added. Again, rent control, along with other aspects of the local regulatory environment, may play a role in the decisions of some landlords who remove properties from rental use. However, the current system of rent control is a balanced one, which--at least in recent years--has allowed rent revenues to rise along with operating costs, and which--in principle--offers opportunities for land-lords to obtain greater rent increases if they are experiencing financial hardship or if they choose to invest in capital improvements.

The units at greatest risk of being removed from the stock--those with very low rents and chronic code viola-tions--qualify for hardship rent increases under the District's regulatory regime, but have not applied for them. Rent control is by no means the primary constraint preventing the owners of these units from raising rents and making property improvements. The administrative and financial burden of the hardship petition process may present a difficult hurdle for these landlords, but their primary problem is that the tenants who occupy their buildings are simply too poor to pay the rent levels required to make maintenance profitable.

Thus, although control has not caused the problems of housing availability and affordability in the District of Columbia, it certainly has not eliminated these problems either. Despite the rent reductions attributable to the existing system of controls, 43 percent of all renters in the District pay more than 30 percent of their income for housing, and about

10 percent pay more than three-quarters of their income for housing, placing them seriously at risk of homelessness. A full solution to the District's shortage of low- and moderate-cost rental housing would require a combination of direct subsidies to poor households, systematic efforts to preserve rental properties currently occupied by low- and moderate-income renters, and production of additional units set aside for needy households.

The remainder of this report presents the data and analysis supporting our conclusions about the impact of rent control in the District of Columbia. We begin by describing the District's rental market, focusing on the characteristics of D.C. renters (chapter 2), on the affordability and adequacy of rental housing (chapter 3), and on the ownership and financial characteristics of the rental stock (chapter 4). Next, the report assesses the role rent control has played in determining market outcomes, first from the tenants' perspective (chapter 5), and then from the landlords' perspective (chapter 6). Finally, the report concludes with a discussion of the implications of these findings in the context of our understanding of how urban housing markets work.

Notes, chapter one

1. For more on trends in rental housing affordability, see Joint Center for Housing Studies, 1989, *The State of the Nation's Housing, 1989*. Cambridge, Mass: Harvard University.

2. See R. Struyk, M. Turner, M. Ueno, 1989, *Future U.S. Housing Policy: Meeting the Demographic Challenge*. Washington, D.C.: Urban Institute Press.

3. See appendix A for more details on the origins and scope of the Institute's rent control study.

4. For an excellent, up-to-date review of the empirical and theoretical literature on rent control, see A. Downs, 1988, *Residential Rent Controls: An Evaluation.* Washington, D.C.: Urban Land Institute.

Chapter Two

DISTRICT OF COLUMBIA RENTERS:
A PROFILE

Almost two-thirds (61 percent) of District of Columbia households are renters--about 157,900 households. Roughly 20 percent of these renter households receive federal or local rent subsidies.[1] This chapter profiles the approximately 129,600 D.C. renter households who are unassisted, since it is these renters whose housing circumstances are most likely to be affected by rent control. The characteristics of these renters are contrasted with those of their suburban counterparts, as well as with those of renters in other U.S. central cities. Data are drawn from The Urban Institute's survey of 3,600 unassisted renter households in D.C. and the surrounding suburbs, from the 1974 American Housing Survey (AHS, conducted by the U.S. Bureau of the Census), and from published AHS tabulations for other metropolitan areas. (See appendix B for more details on sampling and survey methodology.)

D.C. RENTERS--CURRENT CHARACTERISTICS

The District's renter population is by no means homogeneous. Instead, it is made up of several distinct groups of households whose composition, life-cycle status, and socioeconomic circumstances differ significantly, and who consequently face very different housing opportunities and housing problems. Figure 2.1 illustrates the relative size of six distinct groups of renter households in the District of Columbia:

1. Nonelderly singles
2. Elderly singles and couples
3. Groups of unrelated adults
4. Nonelderly couples
5. Husband-wife families with children
6. Female-headed families with children

Nonelderly singles and groups of unrelated adults--who together account for about 57 percent of all D.C. households--form an ethnically diverse and relatively affluent segment of the population. Many of these young renters are relative newcomers to the D.C. area who will participate only temporarily in the District's rental market. In contrast, families and elderly households who rent housing in the District are predominantly black, generally poorer, and much more likely to be long-term residents of the city (see table 2.1).

Table 2.1   D.C. RENTER ATTRIBUTES BY LIFE-CYCLE GROUP, 1987

	Median Income($)	Black (%)	Newcomers to D.C. (%)
Nonelderly singles	20,000	52.2	36.9
Adult groups	30,000	41.3	52.3
Elderly	13,000	64.9	2.9
Nonelderly couples	22,000	75.7	23.7
Husband-wife families	23,000	83.9	20.7
Female-headed families	15,000	91.2	10.5

FIGURE 2.1 D.C. RENTER HOUSEHOLDS: LIFE-CYCLE GROUPS, 1987 (percent)

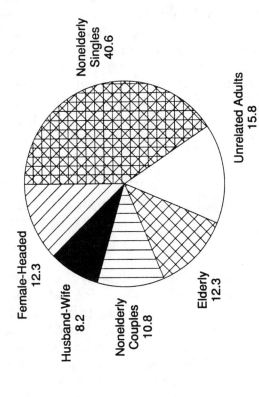

Nonelderly Singles 40.6

Unrelated Adults 15.8

Elderly 12.3

Nonelderly Couples 10.8

Husband-Wife 8.2

Female-Headed 12.3

Source: 1987 Urban Institute "Tenant Survey."

The presence of these very different segments in the D.C. rental housing market is largely explained by the widespread U.S. preference for homeownership. Almost all households who do not view their current living situation as temporary want to become homeowners if they can afford it. Thus, owner-occupancy rates among families and elderly people are very high, and households who remain renters either choose to do so because they expect to change their living arrangements relatively soon, or are forced to do so because they cannot afford homeownership. As a result, in Washington--as in other central cities throughout the U.S.--the majority of renters have low to moderate incomes,[2] with the exception of the young singles and groups of unrelated adults, who are relative short-timers in the local rental housing market.

D.C. RENTERS IN THE METROPOLITAN AND NATIONAL CONTEXT

District renters differ significantly from their counterparts in surrounding suburban jurisdictions with respect to race and household composition. Only about one-third of suburban renters are black, compared to almost two-thirds of the D.C. renter population. As in D.C., more than half of all suburban renters are childless households. But in the suburbs, the share of nonelderly singles is considerably smaller than in the District, while the share of adult groups is much larger. This is probably explained, in part, by differences between the D.C. and suburban rental housing stock. Specifically, over half of all D.C. rental units are small apartments (three rooms or less), while the majority (almost three-quarters) of suburban units have four or more rooms. Thus, young single people in the metropolitan area who decide to share housing are more likely to find large rental units in the suburbs, while those who prefer to live alone are more likely to remain in the District.

The biggest difference between D.C. and suburban renters is their incomes. Across all six life-cycle groups, suburban renters are more affluent than their central city counterparts (see table 2.2). The median income among all suburban renters is about $35,000, compared to $20,000 among District renters; and 20 percent of suburban renters earn over $50,000, compared to only 6 percent of renters in the District. Although the suburban income advantage is far more pronounced for families with children than for childless households, the differential cannot be dismissed as simply a reflection of a different mix of household types; it applies to all life-cycle groups.

Table 2.2   MEDIAN INCOME OF D.C. AND SUBURBAN RENTERS BY LIFE-CYCLE GROUP, 1987

	D.C. ($)	Suburbs ($)
Nonelderly Singles	20,000	25,000
Adult groups	30,000	35,000
Elderly	13,000	15,000
Nonelderly Couples	22,000	40,000
Husband-wife families	23,000	33,000
Female-headed families	15,000	30,000

Although D.C. renters are much poorer than their counterparts in the surrounding suburbs, they are relatively affluent in comparison with other U.S. central cities. Table 2.3 compares the characteristics of the D.C. renter population with those of all U.S. central cities and to eight specific central cities in the Northeast and Middle-Atlantic states.

Table 2.3   D.C. AND OTHER U.S. CENTRAL CITY RENTERS: DEMOGRAPHIC AND ECONOMIC CHARACTERISTICS

	Number of Households	Renters (%)	Among Renter Households						
			Black (%)	Elderly (%)	Singles (%)	With Children (%)	Average Household Size	Percentage with more than High School Education	Median Income ($)
U.S. central city total (1983)	27,257,000	50.8	32.1	16.5	37.8	31.4	1.9	36.1	11,500
Atlanta (1982)	179,700	65.6	65.6	17.1	39.5	30.6	1.9	38.3	9,500
Baltimore (1983)	305,800	51.5	59.6	19.1	35.5	33.0	2.1	21.0	9,900
Hartford (1983)	54,900	73.8	35.0	17.5	39.6	28.4	1.9	23.0	10,900
Philadelphia (1982)	688,300	39.3	45.1	15.9	38.3	31.6	1.9	30.6	9,500
Pittsburgh (1981)	179,800	47.1	32.6	17.0	46.3	25.1	1.6	37.1	9,700
Rochester (1982)	101,700	52.3	26.5	13.2	44.2	27.4	1.7	36.2	10,100
Boston (1981)	245,400	59.1	26.7	17.7	40.6	24.9	1.8	42.1	10,900
Newark (1981)	120,800	77.1	64.9	14.4	28.3	40.8	2.4	28.2	8,700
D.C. (1981)	280,400	63.3	71.9	14.5	45.1	29.3	1.7	41.6	13,600

Source: Published American Housing Survey volumes, 1981-83. Washington, D.C.: U.S. Bureau of the Census.

On average, D.C. renters appear to be better educated and substantially more affluent than renters in other central cities. In part, this is explained by the somewhat unusual composition of the city's renter population. Specifically, it seems likely that the District's universities and its unique job market attract large numbers of affluent short-timers. This is evidenced by the high proportion of D.C. renters who are nonelderly singles and the low proportion who are families with children. As discussed earlier, many of the District's affluent short-timers choose to rent because their current living arrangements are temporary. Their high socio-economic status boosts the average for the population as a whole. Still, even when when we compare D.C. renters who are elderly and those with children to similar households in other cities, D.C. renters enjoy a marked income advantage.

RECENT TRENDS

The size of the District's renter population declined substantially during the second half of the 1970s, a decline that appears to have continued--though at a slower rate--into the early 1980s. The decrease occurred at the same time that the number of homeowners in the District was increasing and, as a result, the share of D.C. households who rent dropped precipitously, from 70 percent in 1974 to about 62 percent today.[3]

At the same time that the District's renter population shrank in size, its composition shifted significantly, to include more young singles and adult groups and fewer families with children (see Figure 2.2).[4] Specifically, the share of non-elderly singles and groups of young adults increased from 42 percent to 57 percent between 1974 and 1987, while the share

FIGURE 2.2 D.C. RENTER HOUSEHOLDS: DEMOGRAPHIC TRENDS, 1974-87

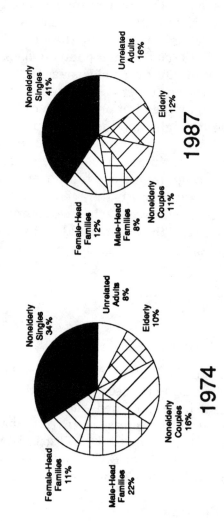

1987

Nonelderly Singles 41%

Unrelated Adults 16%

Elderly 12%

Nonelderly Couples 11%

Male-Head Families 8%

Female-Head Families 12%

1974

Nonelderly Singles 34%

Unrelated Adults 8%

Elderly 10%

Nonelderly Couples 16%

Male-Head Families 22%

Female-Head Families 11%

Sources: 1984 American Housing Survey, and Urban Institute "Tenant Survey."

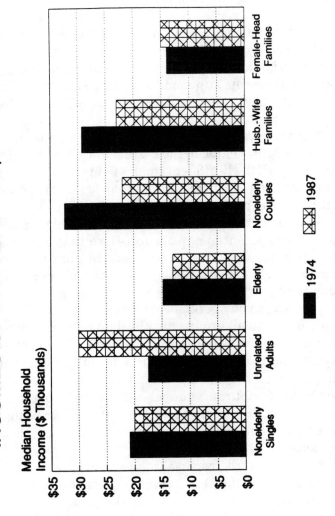

FIGURE 2.3 CHANGES IN MEDIAN REAL INCOMES OF D.C. RENTERS, 1974 & 1987

Note: Median household income is in 1987 dollars.

of families with children declined from 33 percent to 20 percent. Moreover, as figure 2.3 illustrates, real incomes (adjusted for inflation) grew among singles and adult groups, but declined among all other types of renter households. In other words, the most affluent segments of the D.C. renter population became larger and even more affluent, while the more permanent core of elderly and family renters became smaller and poorer.

This shift resulted from two important trends, neither of which has been unique to the District of Columbia. First, the number of relatively affluent singles living alone or in groups of unrelated adults increased in urban areas throughout the U.S.; and second, middle-income families achieved homeownership and/or suburbanization at a high rate. Thus, the District's renter population--like that of U.S. cities generally--is increasingly composed of poor families and elderly people who cannot afford to become homeowners, along with more affluent singles and adult groups who are not yet ready to buy permanent homes.

By contrast, all groups of suburban renters experienced real income gains between 1974 and 1987. The increase was largest among unrelated individuals, and smallest among female-headed families and the elderly. But for every group, the share of suburban households in the poorest income category declined between 1974 and 1987, leaving these renters substantially better off economically than their D.C. counterparts.

Both the overall drop in absolute numbers and the shift in composition of the D.C. renter population reflect major national trends as well as local market conditions. Nationwide demographic trends, combined with compelling incentives for homeownership that prevailed during the late 1970s, produced similar changes in the size of the renter population of many U.S. cities. And nonelderly singles--living alone and in groups--have been one of the fastest growing segments of the population throughout the nation over the last decade and a half.

The first important trend has been a widespread increase in the number of affluent young adults postponing marriage and either living alone or in groups. It makes sense for households in this group to choose rental status despite their high income levels, because their household arrangements are temporary. At the same time, the second half of the 1970s witnessed widespread increases in homeownership rates because federal income tax benefits and high inflation rates made homeownership exceedingly attractive. Throughout the U.S., an increasing share of middle-income households who could do so became homeowners. Thus, the number of renter households in many other U.S. central cities either declined or grew at a slower rate than the number of home-owners. And the growth in renter incomes was generally very modest during the late 1970s and early 1980s, especially in cities that lost renter population.

During the early to mid-1980s, high interest rates, lower inflation, and changes in the tax incentives for home-ownership substantially reduced the pressures for households to become owner-occupants. This change in national economic conditions probably explains the recent stabilization of the District's renter population, and has resulted in intensified pressure on the available stock of rental housing in D.C. Households of all types, but particularly young singles, groups of unrelated adults, and young families with children are now postponing homeownership, and are more likely to remain renters longer.

Notes, chapter two

1. Our estimate of the total number of renter households in the District is derived as follows: The American Housing Survey (AHS) of the U.S. Bureau of the Census estimates that there were 160,400 rental units in D.C. in 1985. Our inventory of additions and losses to the rental stock between 1985 and 1987 yielded about 1,600 additions by 1987, to yield a 1987 total of 162,000 rental units. According to the AHS, the rental vacancy rate (units vacant for rent divided by total renter occupied and vacant for rent) for D.C. was 2.51 percent in 1985. We have assumed that this rate remained essentially the same between 1985 and 1987, for a total of 157,900 D.C. renter households.

2. For purposes of this analysis, we have defined the following income categories, based on 1987 annual incomes: less than $15,000--low income or poor; between $15,000 and $25,000--moderate income; between $25,000 and $35,000--lower-middle income; between $35,000 and $50,000--upper-middle income; and over $50,000--high income or affluent.

3. Trends in the size of the D.C. renter population were obtained from published American Housing Survey data, which indicate that the number of D.C. renters declined from 180,000 in 1974, to 174,900 in 1977, and to 159,900 in 1981. At the same time, the number of homeowners in the District increased from 77,700 in 1974, to 81,600 in 1977, and to 92,600 in 1981.

4. Using data on magnetic tape from the 1974 AHS for the Washington, D.C., metropolitan area, we were able to classify households and their housing conditions in 1974 using the same definitions that applied to our 1987 survey data.

Chapter Three

RENTAL HOUSING AFFORDABILITY
AND ADEQUACY IN D.C.

The central objective of the District's rent control program is to protect tenants from excessive rents and rent increases. In fact, affordability is the most widespread housing problem facing District renters, especially those of limited means. This chapter draws on both our 1987 survey of 3,000 District renters and the 1974 American Housing Survey (AHS) to describe current housing conditions and recent trends in D.C. and the surrounding suburbs. In addition, we present data from published AHS tabulations on comparable trends in other U.S. central cities.

HOUSING PROBLEMS FOR D.C. RENTERS

More than half of D.C. renters face serious housing problems of affordability, adequacy, or crowding. As figure 3.1 illustrates, only 44 percent of D.C. renters live in fully adequate units and spend 30 percent or less of their income for rent and utilities. The biggest problem facing D.C. renters is housing affordability. More than two-fifths (about 43 percent) of all D.C. renters spend over 30 percent of their income for housing. Most of these households are paying high rents to live in fully adequate housing, but a significant minority pay too much and still live in overcrowded or physically deficient units.

Figure 3.1   D.C. RENTER HOUSEHOLDS: PERCENT
              WITH HOUSING PROBLEMS, 1987

Households with 1 or more problems		*56.0*
Households with excessive rent burden		*42.4*
Excessive rent burden only	31.6	
Excessive rent and deficient units	7.8	
Excessive rent and crowed	2.2	
Excessive rent, deficient, and crowded	0.8	
Households in deficient units		*20.5*
Deficient only	11.2	
Deficient and excessive rent	7.8	
Deficient and crowded	0.7	
Deficient, excessive rent, and crowded	0.8	
Households in overcrowded units		*5.3*
Crowded only	1.6	
Crowded and excessive rent	2.2	
Crowded and deficient	0.7	
Crowded, excessive rent, and deficient	0.8	

Source: 1987 Urban Institute "Tenant Survey."

Even more dramatic than the large share of renters spending over 30 percent of income for housing is the share of households with extremely high rent burdens. A full one-quarter of District renters report that they spend over 45 percent of their income for housing, and more than 10 percent pay over three quarters of their income for housing. This latter group of renters can be thought of as a group "at risk" of becoming homeless.

Affordability problems are directly related to household incomes, as shown by figure 3.2. It is only within the poorest income group (annual incomes under $15,000) that a majority of households bear excessive rent burdens. None of the most affluent renter households have rent burdens over 45 percent, compared to 60 percent of the poorest households. And even among moderate-income renters (annual incomes between $15,000 and $24,000) the share paying more than 35 percent of income for housing drops to less than 20 percent.

In addition to the severe problem of housing affordability, a significant share of the District's rental housing stock is physically deficient. In fact, roughly one-fifth of all households report at least one structural deficiency or three serious maintenance problems. And the problem of physically deficient housing does not appear to be limited to any particular segment of the District's rental market. Housing quality is somewhat sensitive to rent levels, with 30 percent of units in the lowest contract rent category (monthly rent under $200) reporting serious deficiencies, compared to only 18 percent of units in the highest contract rent category (monthly rent of $900 or more). However, between these two extremes, the rate of deficiencies remains remarkably close to the citywide average (see table 3.1).

Overcrowding is a much less significant problem for D.C.'s overall rental market, but nevertheless is a serious problem for families with children. Only about 5 percent of all renter households live in units with more than one person

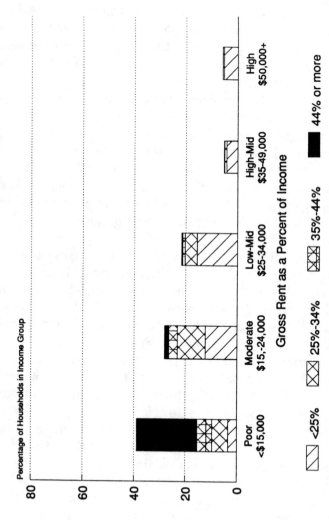

FIGURE 3.2 D.C. RENTER HOUSEHOLDS:
RENT BURDEN BY INCOME GROUP, 1987

Source: 1987 Urban Institute "Tenant Survey."

Table 3.1   INCIDENCE OF DEFICIENCIES BY
              CONTRACT RENT

All renter households	20.5
Monthly contract rent:	
Less than $200	29.7
$200 - $299	20.4
$300 - $399	20.2
$400 - $499	22.1
$500 - $599	19.0
$600 - $699	18.7
$700 - $899	19.9
$900 or more	17.6

per room. But almost 20 percent of the families who have
children live in overcrowded conditions (see table 3.2). The
problem of crowding is most severe for large families; over
half the families with three or more children are overcrowded. Higher income and higher rent can help households avoid crowded conditions, but even middle-income
renters with three or more children have more than a 50
percent chance of being overcrowded. The primary problem,
clearly, is a shortage of large rental units in the District's
rental market--at virtually all rent levels.

Table 3.2   INCIDENCE OF OVERCROWDING BY
              LIFE-CYCLE STATUS (%)

All renter households	5.3
Nonelderly singles	0.0
Unrelated adults	6.2
Elderly	0.4
Nonelderly couples	6.0
Husband-wife families	20.7
Female-headed families	15.4

D.C. RENTAL HOUSING CONDITIONS IN THE METROPOLITAN AND NATIONAL CONTEXT

Overall, a somewhat smaller share of suburban households faces serious housing problems as compared to D.C. renters (see table 3.3). About half of all suburban renters have no housing problems, compared to only 44 percent of D.C. renters. This difference is entirely attributable to the fact that affordability problems are substantially less prevalent among suburban renters than in the District. Only about one-quarter of suburban renters pay more than 30 percent of their income for housing, compared to 43 percent in D.C.

Housing quality problems actually seem to be more prevalent in the suburbs than in the District. In fact, 27 percent of suburban renters (compared to only about 20 percent of D.C. renters) report physical deficiencies in their units. And finally, a slightly a smaller share of suburban renters are overcrowded. Less than 3 percent of suburban renters live in units with more than one person per room, compared to over 5 percent in D.C.

Table 3.3   D.C. AND SUBURBAN RENTER HOUSEHOLDS: PERCENTAGE WITH HOUSING PROBLEMS, 1987

	D.C. ($)	Suburbs ($)
Households with one or more problems	56.0	49.3
Households with excessive rent burden	42.4	26.5
Households in deficient units	20.5	27.3
Households in overcrowded units	5.3	5.2

Source: 1987 Urban Institute Tenant Survey.

The lower incidence of excessive cost burden in the suburbs is not explained by lower rent levels, but by higher income levels. Suburban rental units are considerably more expensive than those inside the District, as shown by figure 3.3. Almost half of D.C. units rent for under $400, compared to less than 5 percent of suburban units. And more than half of suburban units rent for over $600, compared to only about 20 percent of D.C. units. In large part, this stems from the fact that suburban rental units are larger than those in D.C. (see figure 3.4). Over half of D.C. units have three rooms or fewer, while almost three-quarters of suburban units have four or more rooms. Because suburban rental housing is larger and more costly than the District's rental stock, the low-income renters who live in the suburbs are more likely than D.C. renters to face severe affordability problems. Among suburban households with annual incomes under $25,000, 76 percent pay over 30 percent of their income for housing, compared to 62 percent in the District.

Although D.C. renters face serious problems of housing affordability, adequacy, and crowding, these problems are actually less severe than those confronting renters in other U.S. central cities. The incidence of housing deficiencies and crowding are about the same in metropolitan areas nationally as in the Washington region, but, as illustrated in table 3.4, affordability problems are considerably worse for renters in many other central cities. This is partially explained by the relatively high incomes of D.C. renters, compared to their counterparts in other central cities. Nevertheless, even among low-income households, D.C. renters have lower average cost burdens than renters in other U.S. central cities.

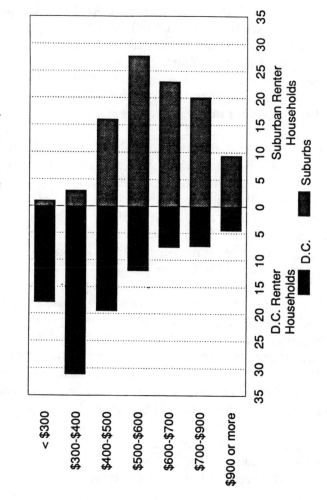

FIGURE 3.3 D.C. AND SUBURBAN RENTERS: GROSS RENTS, 1987 (percent)

Source: 1987 Urban Institute "Tenant Survey."

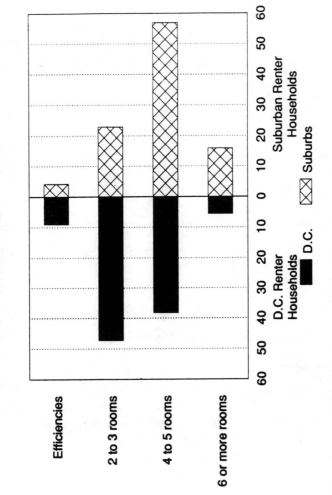

FIGURE 3.4 D.C. AND SUBURBAN RENTERS
UNIT MIX, 1987 (percent)

Source: 1987 Urban Institute "Tenant Survey."

Table 3.4   D.C. AND OTHER CENTRAL CITIES: HOUSING
                AFFORDABILITY AND CROWDING

	Rent ($)	Income ($)	Rent Burden (%)	Percentage With More Than 1 Person Per Room
U.S. central city total (1983)	243	11,500	31	6.5
Atlanta (1982	195	9,500	30	4.5
Baltimore (1983)	214	9,900	31	4.5
Hartford (1983)	218	10,900	32	5.5
Philadelphia (1982)	217	9,500	34	5.5
Pittsburgh (1981)	216	9,700	29	5.1
Rochester (1982)	221	10,100	34	3.7
Boston (1981)	251	10,900	31	5.1
Newark (1981)	214	8,700	31	13.6
Washington, D.C. (1981)	226	13,600	23	6.6

Source: Published American Housing Survey volumes, 1981-83.
Washington, D.C.: U.S. Bureau of the Census.

RECENT TRENDS IN AFFORDABILITY
AND ADEQUACY

Housing problems have worsened considerably in the District since 1974. The share of D.C. renters with one or more serious housing problems increased from about 50 percent in 1974 to 56 percent in 1987. This rise is wholly attributable to increasing rent burdens, with the share of renters paying more than 30 percent of income for housing increasing from 27 percent to 42 percent between 1974 and 1987. The share of D.C. renters living in deficient units actually declined, from 27 percent in 1974 to 21 percent in 1987. And the share of overcrowded households stayed essentially the same over the 1974-87 period.

In the early 1970s, housing cost burdens were substantially lower for all income groups in the District. Virtually all of the households paying more than 30 percent of their income for housing were in the lowest income group, but even among poor renters, most paid less than 30 percent. Today, the vast majority of poor renters pay excessive housing cost burdens, and even among moderate- and middle-income renters, the share spending more than 30 percent of their income for housing is significant.

Suburban renters have not experienced the same dramatic increase in affordability problems, primarily because income growth among suburban renters has more than kept pace with rising rent levels. Overall, the share of suburban renters paying more than 30 percent of their income for rent only increased slightly over the 1974-87 period--from just over 20 percent to about 25 percent. Although rents have risen more rapidly in the suburbs than in D.C., the incomes of suburban renters have more than kept pace, whereas those of D.C.

Table 3.5   D.C. AND OTHER CENTRAL CITIES: RECENT
            TRENDS IN HOUSING AFFORDABILITY

| | Average Annual Percentage Change in | | Median Rent Burden | |
	Rent	Income	Mid-1970s (%)	Early 1980s
U.S. central city total (1983)	9.43%	5.34%		31%
Atlanta (1982	10.24	6.04	24	30
Baltimore (1983)	8.86	3.85	25	31
Hartford (1983)	8.97	6.88	28	32
Philadelphia (1982)	9.87	5.34	26	34
Pittsburgh (1981)	11.48	6.36	24	29
Rochester (1982)	7.50	5.38	28	34
Boston (1981)	9.40	5.69	28	31
Newark (1981)	6.99	3.15	26	31
Washington, D.C. (1981)	7.77	6.08	21	23

Source: Published American Housing Survey volumes, 1981-83.
Washington, D.C.: U.S. Bureau of the Census.

renters have fallen short. Specifically, gross rents in the
District have grown at an average annual rate of 7.8 percent
since 1974, while D.C. renter incomes only rose 6.1 percent
annually. In contrast, suburban rent levels have climbed 8.6
percent annually since 1974, but this increase has been
matched by growth in suburban renters' incomes.

Renters in other U.S. central cities have experienced even
more dramatic increases in affordability problems than have
D.C. renters. As shown in table 3.5, income gains among
renter households have consistently fallen short of rent
inflation. And as a result, the share of renters paying more
than 30 percent of their income for housing has increased by

four or more percentage points in several cities, and often approaches one-third of all central city renters. The more moderate experience of D.C. renters is attributable both to their slightly above-average rate of income growth and to a below-average rate of rent inflation.

CHANGES IN THE RENTAL HOUSING STOCK

Over time, change occurs in the availability, adequacy, and affordability of rental housing as units are added to and lost from the rental inventory. New construction and substantial rehabilitation are the most obvious sources of change in the housing stock, but a variety of other supply mechanisms allow property owners to adjust the rental housing supply over time. Figure 3.5 illustrates the potential components of change in the rental housing inventory. The number of units available for rent can be increased by:

- New construction;

- Conversion of structures from commercial or industrial use to residential use;

- Rehabilitation of boarded-up properties;

- Conversion of owner-occupied housing to rental use; and

- Subdivision of existing rental units into a larger number of units.

Correspondingly, the number of units available for rent can be reduced by:

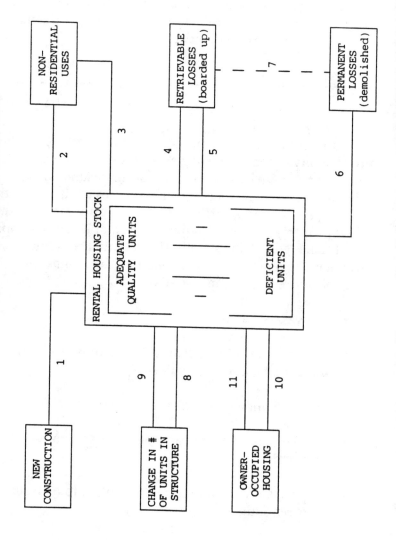

FIGURE 3.5   COMPONENTS OF INVENTORY CHANGE MODEL

- Conversion of structures from residential to commercial or industrial use;

- Deterioration or disinvestment, which causes a unit to be removed from the habitable inventory;

- Demolition of a property--either one in active use or one that had previously been boarded up;

- Conversion of rental housing to owner-occupancy; and

- Merger of two or more rental units into fewer units.

During the 1970s, the total number of rental units in the District declined substantially--from 199,100 in 1970 to 170,500 in 1981. This decline occurred despite new rental construction averaging about 740 units per year, and is attributable to the removal of at least 3,340 units from the rental stock annually during that period. Two key, demand-side forces explain the 15 percent decline in the size of the District's rental housing inventory between 1970 and 1981. First, as discussed earlier, the total number of middle- and upper-income renters in the District dropped substantially, owing to the loss of households to the suburbs and the rising rate of homeownership among those remaining in the District. At the same time, among renters for whom the option of homeownership was unaffordable, incomes failed to keep pace with inflation. Thus, the top end of the rental market was eroded by a decline in the aggregate level of demand, while the bottom end of the market was eroded by a decline in the real purchasing power of low- and moderate-income renters.

The 1970s represent a period when the opportunities for both homeownership and suburbanization were unusually attractive, not only in the District of Columbia but throughout the country. High marginal tax rates and rapid inflation made homeownership increasingly attractive to anyone who could afford a down payment, and the suburbs were more hospitable to minorities than they had been at any time in the past. Thus, the aggregate level of demand for rental housing declined substantially. Roughly one-quarter of the net decline in the rental housing stock was matched by a drop in the total number of households living in the District, and almost half was matched by conversions to homeownership.[1] The fact that rental vacancy rates remained constant between 1974 and 1981 testifies to the fact that the total supply of rental housing in D.C. declined by roughly the same amount as the total level of demand. Moreover, as figure 3.6 shows, this pattern was by no means unique to the District of Columbia--during the 1970s central cities throughout the country lost renter households (and housing units) to the combined attractions of homeownership and suburbanization.

During the first half of the 1980s, the decline in demand for rental housing in the District slowed considerably. In other words, demand for rental housing in the District began to stabilize during the first half of the 1980s, probably because rising interest rates, lower inflation, and reductions in marginal tax rates all contributed to make homeownership much less affordable relative to rental housing. However, while the loss of renter households slowed considerably during the 1980s, the supply of rental units continued to decline at a somewhat faster pace. The result was a dramatic drop in the rental vacancy rate, from 6.2 percent in 1981 to 2.5 percent in 1985.

Since 1985, the District's rental housing stock has actually started growing again, both because units are being removed from rental use at a much lower rate than in the 1970s and

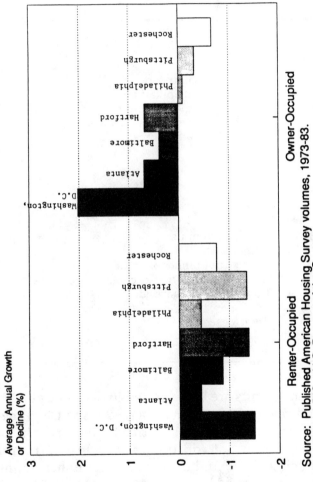

FIGURE 3.6 U.S. CENTRAL CITIES:
TRENDS IN THE HOUSING STOCK, 1970-83

Average Annual Growth or Decline (%)

Renter-Occupied   Owner-Occupied

Source: Published American Housing Survey volumes, 1973-83.
Washington, D.C.: U.S. Bureau of the Census

Table 3.6   ADDITIONS TO AND LOSSES FROM D.C. RENTAL
HOUSING STOCK, MAY 1985-APRIL 1987

	May 1985- April 1987
Additions	
New construction	1,003
Substantial rehabilitation	1,094
Change in number of units	70
Conversion from owner-occupied	106
Conversion from nonresidential	398
Total additions	2,621
Losses	
Removed from use	152
Demolished	11
Change in number of units	29
Conversion to owner-occupied	760
Conversion to nonresidential	38
Total losses	990
Net Change	1,631

because units are being added to the stock at a higher rate.
This reversal represents a lagged response to the renewed
demand for rental housing that began earlier in the decade.
An inventory of additions to and losses from the rental
housing stock[2] indicates that the number of units on the
market increased by 1,631 between May 1, 1985, and April 30,
1987 (table 3.6). Although new construction remained at
roughly the same level as in the 1970s, the rental housing
stock increased by about 800 units annually, because very few

units were removed from the rental stock and because a relatively large number of units was added to the rental inventory through renovations or conversions from non-residential uses.

Despite the high rate of increase in the District's rental housing stock during recent years, fully half of the recent additions may not remain in the rental stock permanently, because they were developed as condominiums that are currently being rented rather than owner-occupied. In fact, the vast majority (81 percent) of condominium units built or renovated between 1985 and 1987 are currently being rented rather than owner-occupied. Thus, developers appear to be aware that the demand for rental housing in the District--especially among the higher income singles and adult groups--is sensitive to the relative attractiveness of owning versus renting. And units that are being added to the rental inventory in response to a resurgence in demand can easily be converted to owner-occupancy in response to renewed pressure for homeownership.

The recent additions to the District's rental housing stock have boosted the size of the inventory, but most do not respond to the needs of the city's low-income renters. During the 1970s, three-quarters of the building permits issued for rental housing construction and substantial renovation were for units subsidized by the federal government. By contrast, between 1980 and 1986, only one-quarter of the rental building permits issued in the District were for subsidized units, reflecting both the virtual elimination of federal housing production programs and the increase in the volume of unassisted rental production in the District.[3]

While most of the units added to the rental stock in recent years are not affordable to low- and moderate-income households, the vast majority of the units lost from the District's rental stock since the early 1970s rented for less than $350 (in 1987 dollars).[4] Thus, the inventory of low-cost rental

Table 3.7   AVAILABILITY OF AFFORDABLE RENTAL UNITS, 1987

	Low Income (< $15,000)	Moderate Income ($15,000-$24,000)
Number of households	49,000	37,000
Number of affordable units	42,000	28,000

units has declined substantially in size, resulting in a serious shortage of housing affordable for the District's low- and moderate-income renters. The resources of these renter groups--particularly the elderly and families with children--are too limited to make the ownership and maintenance of low- and moderate-cost rental properties profitable. As a result, the number of unsubsidized rental units that are affordable for low- and moderate-income households in the District falls far short of the need for these units (see table 3.7). In all, there are about 25 percent more low- and moderate-income renters in the District than there are units that these households can reasonably afford.

Notes, chapter three

1. This analysis of change in the rental housing inventory during the 1970s is based on published AHS data on rental and owner-occupied units in the Washington, D.C., metropolitan area.

2. See appendix B for details on the inventory of 1985-87 additions to and losses from the District's rental stock.

3. These estimates are obtained from tabulations of building permits in the Washington, D.C., metropolitan area assembled by

the U.S. Department of Housing and Urban Development (HUD) field office. Note that, since 1984, local subsidy programs have played a small but significant role in the production of D.C. rental housing, accounting for half of the subsidized units that received building permits between 1984 and 1986--or about 10 percent of all rental units for which building permits were issued.

4. Based on published AHS data on rent levels of units removed from the rental inventory.

Chapter Four

THE D.C. RENTAL STOCK: A FINANCIAL PROFILE

The implications of rent control in any urban housing market depend not only on the characteristics of renters and their housing needs but also on the characteristics of landlords and the financial viability of their rental housing investments. This chapter describes the ownership and financial characteristics of controlled rental units in the District of Columbia. The findings presented here were compiled from financial statements (from D.C. government files) for 814 randomly selected properties, as well as from responses to a questionnaire soliciting additional factual and attitudinal data from owners or managers of 244 of these properties. For details on sampling and data collection, see appendix B.[1]

OWNERSHIP FORM AND MOTIVATIONS

Controlled rental units in the District are divided roughly evenly among three basic forms of ownership--individual owners, partnerships and joint ventures, and, finally, corporations and trusts. Partnerships and joint ventures account for two-fifths of the District's controlled units; individuals own about one-third of the units; and corporations and trusts account for the remaining one-fourth.

Both partnerships and corporate owners tend to have substantial holdings in D.C. rental units, while individuals are much more diverse in terms of the size of their total holdings. The vast majority of partnership- and corporate-owned units--79 percent and 85 percent respectively--are held by owners whose total D.C. holdings exceed 50 units. Almost half of individually owned units are held by owners with more than 50 units altogether, and the remainder are roughly evenly distributed between owners with small and medium-sized holdings.

Thus, we can define six distinct types of D.C. property owners, based on ownership form and the size of their total rental holdings:

1. Individual owners with small D.C. holdings--fewer than 10 rental units overall;

2. Individual owners with medium holdings--10 to 49 rental units;

3. Individual owners with large holdings--50 or more rental units;

4. Partnerships and joint ventures with small to medium holdings--fewer than 50 units;

5. Partnerships and joint ventures with large holdings; and

6. Corporations.

Figure 4.1 shows the proportion of the rental market controlled by each of these six ownership types. Clearly, the lion's share of controlled units in D.C. is held by large owners--26 percent by corporations, 34 percent by large

FIGURE 4.1 CONTROLLED RENTAL UNITS: SHARE OF UNITS BY OWNERSHIP TYPE

(Numbers in parentheses after each category correspond list of classifications in the text.)

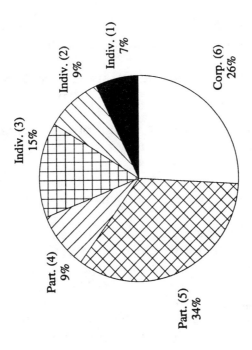

Indiv. (3)
15%

Indiv. (2)
9%

Indiv. (1)
7%

Corp. (6)
26%

Part. (4)
9%

Part. (5)
34%

Source: 1987 Urban Institute "Housing Provider Survey."

partnerships, and 15 percent by large individual owners. Small individual owners account for only a small share (7 percent) of the controlled rental units in D.C.

Controlled landlords were asked several questions regarding their attitudes toward investment in D.C. rental property:

- Is owning, developing, or managing real estate your principal business or source of income?

- What would you say are your main reasons for investing in this rental property?

- Are you likely to sell this property within the next five years? If so, why?

- Do you expect to invest in District rental housing in the future? If not, why not?

Table 4.1 summarizes their responses to these questions. Owners of about two-thirds (64.8 percent) of the District's controlled rental units own, develop, or manage real estate as their principal business or source of income. For most owners (accounting for three-quarters [76.1 percent] of controlled units), investment in residential real estate was motivated primarily by the cash flow it generates, although property appreciation was also an important inducement--cited as a primary reason for investment by owners of about one-third (32.9 percent) of controlled rental units. Tax incentives were considered of primary importance by owners of only a small share of controlled rental units (16.8 percent).

Owners of only one-third (33.9 percent) of the District's controlled stock expected to sell their units within the next five years. The primary reason given by most of these owners (60.6 percent) was low profitability relative to other invest-

Table 4.1   ATTITUDES AND INTENTIONS OF D.C. RENTAL
PROPERTY OWNERS, 1987

	Percentage of Controlled Units
OWNING, DEVELOPING, OR MANAGING REAL ESTATE IS OWNER'S PRINCIPAL BUSINESS OR SOURCE OF INCOME.	**64.8**
Reasons for investing in D.C. Rental Housing	
Revenues from the property supplement: income each month.	76.1
Owner expects to sell the property for more than he paid for it.	32.9
Owner could extract equity through refinancing.	19.1
Owning this property reduces tax liability.	16.8
OWNER LIKELY TO SELL THIS PROPERTY WITHIN THE NEXT FIVE YEARS.	**33.9**
Reasons for Planning to Sell:	
The value of the property has risen and owner wants to take advantage of the capital gain.	21.7
The value of the property is declining and owner cannot afford to retain it.	19.9
Profits from this investment are not as high as owner could earn from other investments.	60.6
Changes in the tax law make this investment less attractive than it once was.	15.3
Owning this property takes up too much time or is too much trouble.	27.7

Table 4.1   Continued

	Percentage of Controlled Units
OWNER DOES NOT EXPECT TO INVEST IN D.C. RENTAL HOUSING IN THE FUTURE.	**80.6**
Reasons for No Further Investment:	
The new federal tax law makes rental real estate a less attractive investment than it was before.	8.0
Property values are not rising rapidly enough to make rental real estate an attractive investment.	9.6
Rents are not high enough to make rental real estate an attractive investment.	45.5
It is too difficult to obtain financing for rental housing investment.	5.5
Owning rental property is too time consuming or too much trouble.	11.4
D.C. regulatory environment makes investment in other jurisdictions more attractive.	50.2

ment opportunities. Smaller, but still significant, numbers of units were likely to be sold because property ownership is too time consuming (27.7 percent), because the owner wanted to realize increases in property value (21.7 percent), or because property values were declining (19.9 percent). Just as tax incentives were cited as a primary motivation by only a minority of owners, changes in the tax treatment of rental housing were cited as a reason for selling only about 15 percent of the time.

Table 4.2A   CONTROLLED RENTAL UNITS: ATTITUDES TOWARD
             INVESTMENT BY OWNERSHIP TYPE

*Is owning, developing, or managing real estate this owner's
principal business or source of income?*

Ownership Type	Percentage Responding Yes
Individual with small holding	4.46
Individual with medium holding	49.79
Individual with large holding	50.65
Partnership with small/medium holding	45.79
Partnership with large holding	72.25
Corporations	78.46

(continued on next page)

Owners of most of the District's controlled rental units
(80.6 percent) did not intend to invest in D.C. rental housing
in the future. The most commonly mentioned concerns were
low rents (45.5 percent) and a regulatory environment (50.2
percent) that makes investments in other jurisdictions more
attractive. Again, changes in federal tax benefits did not
appear to be a central consideration for most owners (8.0
percent), and neither low property appreciation nor
unavailability of financing were cited as problems more than
10 percent of the time.

Attitudes and plans regarding investment in D.C. rental
housing vary substantially among the different types of
property owners, as illustrated by table 4.2. In general,
smaller owners--particularly individuals--are less likely to be
real estate professionals, more inclined to sell their current

Table 4.2B   CONTROLLED RENTAL UNITS: ATTITUDES TOWARD INVESTMENT BY OWNERSHIP TYPE

	Primary Investment Reason	Percentage Likely to Sell	Primary Reason for Selling	Percentage Unlikely to Invest	Primary Reason for Not Investing
Individual with small holding	Tax benefit	51.58	Property appreciation	95.54	New federal tax law
Individual with medium holding	Lower tax liability	55.07	Depreciating property value	92.81	Regulatory environment
Individual with large holding	Income supplement	19.33	Low Profit	78.58	Time consuming
Partnership with small/medium holding	Property appreciation	50.98	Appreciating value	80.10	Depreciating value
Partnership with large holding	Property appreciation	38.45	Time consuming	76.84	Low rent
Corporations	Refinancing	25.59	Low profit	81.02	Low rent

Source: 1987 Urban Institute Provider Survey.

holdings, and less inclined to invest in the future. The primary reason given by most of the small owners who do not intend to invest further in the future is the recent federal tax reform, rather than local market or regulatory conditions. By contrast, large property owners--who account for the vast majority of controlled units in the District--are the least inclined to sell and are somewhat more willing to invest in D.C. rental housing in the future. But among the large owners who do not intend to invest in the future, local market and regulatory conditions, rather than federal tax changes, are most often cited as primary concerns.

FINANCIAL CONDITIONS AMONG CONTROLLED RENTAL UNITS

In 1985, the average controlled rental unit in the District of Columbia generated annual revenues of $4,170 and incurred $3,523 in operating expenditures and interest payments. Thus, as illustrated by the pro forma financial statement presented in table 4.3, the average unit produced an annual net income of $647 in 1985--about 4.8 percent of current equity.[2]

Financial returns to investment in D.C. rental property vary considerably with both ownership type and property conditions. In general, owners with large holdings of D.C. rental units--including large individual owners, large partnerships, and corporate investors--receive average annual cash returns of about 7 percent. For the average unit owned by small individual owners, expenditures actually exceed revenues, yielding a small *negative* return on an annual basis. In fact, the vast majority (97.2 percent) of units owned by small individuals generate negative cash returns.

How can we explain this low level of cash return among the units owned by small individual investors? The answer appears to lie in the types of properties these investors own. The majority of units owned by small individuals (91.6 percent) are in properties with four units or less--63 percent in three- to four-unit buildings and 28 percent in single-family houses and duplexes. Both of these categories of small properties generate low cash returns, regardless of the type of owner, but for somewhat different reasons.

Single-family homes and duplex units have very high assessed values on average ($60,534 per unit) and correspondingly high encumbrances ($27,140 per unit). These units also generate above-average revenues--$4,709 per unit annually. Nevertheless, on average, total expenditures exceed total revenues by about $200 annually. The largest contributors to operating costs for these units are interest payments, property taxes, fees, and insurance, all of which are directly tied to assessed property values and to the level of encumbrances. Thus, the low cash returns characteristic of single-family homes and duplexes can be attributed to their high assessed values and encumbrances, which, in turn, affect the level of expenditures.

Given the high values and revenues generated by single-family and duplex units, their low rates of cash return clearly do not reflect their real economic value to investors. In fact, as we have seen, federal tax benefits constitute a primary investment motive for small-scale owners, and--among those who expect to sell their units--realization of capital gains is a central factor. Thus, to accurately measure the profitability of investment, we need to incorporate both expected property appreciation and federal income tax benefits.

Indeed, when we incorporate property appreciation into the pro forma financial statement of the average single-family or duplex unit, return on equity becomes substantially positive. More specifically, between 1982 and 1987, the

Table 4.3   CONTROLLED RENTAL UNITS: AVERAGE 1985
             FINANCIAL PRO FORMA

Revenues

Potential rent revenue	$4,293	
Other income	+ $93	
Total potential revenue		$4,386
Vacancy losses	- $150	
Uncontrolled rents	- $66	
Total actual revenue		$4,170

Expenditures

Service and maintenance	$606	
Administrative	+ $290	
Utilities	+ $984	
Operating	+ $442	
Fees and insurance	+ $225	
Property taxes	+ $281	
Management fees	+ $136	
Total operating costs		$2,964
Interest payments	+ $559	
Total expenditure (net of principle repayment)		$3,523

Value, Debt, and Equity

Assessed value	$22,935	
Encumbrances	- $9,481	
Equity		$13,454
Net income/equity		4.8

Source: 1985 D.C. Department of Consumer and Regulatory Affairs
(DCRA)

average assessed value of rented single-family homes and duplexes in the District increased by about 4 percent annually. For the average controlled rental unit in a single-family house or duplex, with a 1985 value of $60,534, a 4 percent rate of appreciation represents an annual gain to the owner of $2,421.[3] Adding this gain to the small negative cash return generated by the unit yields a total return on equity of 6.8 percent.

And, at least until 1986, this return was essentially tax free. Prior to the federal tax reform of 1986, owners of rental property could deduct operating costs, interest payments, and depreciation from the income generated by rental units, and the ultimate gains in property value were taxed at a substantially lower rate than ordinary income. For the average single-family or duplex unit, this treatment produces an after-tax return on equity of about 10 percent (see appendix C for the assumptions underlying our tax calculations). Thus, as small individual owners suggested in response to our attitudinal questions, controlled rental units in the smallest properties (single-family houses and duplexes) provide attractive investment opportunities because of the expected gains in property value and because the overall return on investment is effectively tax free.

Individual owners of three- to four-unit properties face somewhat different circumstances. These units have substantially lower assessed values (averaging $22,564 per unit) and corresponding encumbrances ($11,583 per unit) than single-family and duplex units. And their potential rent revenues are the lowest of all property types--only $3,434 per unit annually on average. The largest cost element for these units is interest payments; none of the other components of operating costs are unusually large relative to other types of units. In essence, the low rent levels generated by these three- to four-unit buildings are simply not sufficient to provide any significant cash flow--particularly owing to their high debt service costs. On average, annual revenues exceed expenditures by only about $100 per unit among three- to four-unit properties.

Again, however, tax benefits and property appreciation are cited as primary investment considerations more often than cash flow by the owners of these units--and for good reason. The average value of three- to four-unit rental properties in the District increased about 8 percent annually between 1982 and 1987. This is a considerably higher rate of appreciation than that of single-family homes and duplexes, and it produces an after-tax return on equity of about 18 percent.

Although most medium- and large-scale property owners do not experience the negative cash returns typical of small individual owners, only about one-quarter of their units yield more than 12 percent cash return on equity annually, and another fifth of their units yield negative returns. On average, large-scale investors appear to enjoy higher cash returns than medium-sized investors, primarily because more of their units are in large buildings (100 units or more). Units in these large properties generate substantially higher revenues (over $4,800 per unit annually) than units in smaller-size categories, and their operating costs are only slightly above average (between $3,500 and $4,000 annually per unit). No single operating cost element stands out as particularly low for units in large properties, suggesting that the largest rental buildings are able to enjoy some general economies of scale. Finally, per-unit property values in large buildings are quite low--about $17,000 compared to the $60,000 per-unit average for single-family homes and duplexes.

Thus, the largest rental properties appear to yield the healthiest cash returns by generating above-average rent revenues with moderate expenditure levels, for a relatively low per-unit equity investment. Landlord responses to attitudinal questions confirm that cash flow is a primary investment motive for owners of the largest properties. How profitable do these units appear to be when one incorporates property appreciation and tax benefits? Between 1982 and 1987, the average value of 20- to 49-unit rental properties in the District increased by about 5 percent annually, while 100- to 249-unit buildings increased in value by about 2 percent per year. The corresponding after-tax returns on equity are about 10 percent for the average unit in a 20- to 49-unit building (compared to a 7.8 percent cash return), and about 12 percent in buildings with 100 to 249 units (compared to a 10.8 percent cash return). Thus, appreciation and tax considerations continue to contribute to the total return on equity for large properties, but cash flow clearly dominates the calculation.

Notes, chapter four

1. Note that D.C. properties that are exempt from rent control are not required to submit financial statements to the D.C. Department of Consumer and Regulatory Affairs (DCRA), and that our analysis of financial and ownership conditions focused exclusively on the controlled portion of the rental inventory.

2. Financial data were obtained from the 1985 "Registration/Claim of Exemption Form" submitted to DCRA. This form does not include principal repayment, and the annual rate of return is computed as: total actual revenue minus total expenditures, divided by assessed value minus encumbrances.

3. Of course, the owner will not realize this gain until the unit is sold or refinanced. However, since data are not available for estimating the number of years owners hold their properties, or for forecasting trends in rents and operating costs, we have used the nominal increase in property value to reflect appreciation gains. This is not the ideal technique for comparing rates of return for competing investment opportunities that have different holding

periods, but it provides reasonable estimates of the approximate return to D.C. landlords from different types of units under differing economic and regulatory conditions.

Chapter Five

IMPACTS OF RENT CONTROL: THE TENANT'S PERSPECTIVE

Rent control has the potential to alter both the demand and supply sides of the market for rental housing. This chapter begins the analysis of the impacts of controls, focusing first on demand-side effects. Using data on the characteristics and price of rental units in D.C. before and after the imposition of controls, we estimate what today's rents would have been in the absence of controls. These estimates provide the starting point for analyzing rent control's effect on the affordability of rental housing, and for understanding tenants' perceptions of rent controls in the District of Columbia.

ESTIMATING RENTS IN THE ABSENCE OF CONTROLS

Estimating what rent levels would have been in the absence of controls constitutes the critical first step in analyzing the impacts of controls on the rental housing market. Our 1987 survey of renter households provides a wealth of information about the characteristics of units on the rental market today, but it obviously cannot tell us what rent levels would have been if rent control had not been implemented. In fact, there is no way to observe empirically what D.C. rents would have been in the absence of controls. We considered three competing strategies for estimating "market" rent levels.

One approach would be to look to the uncontrolled units in the District's housing stock to determine what market conditions would be in the absence of controls. However, the exempt portion of D.C.'s rental housing stock is small, and differs systematically in several important respects from the much larger stock of controlled units. Moreover, there are good reasons to suspect that rent control has affected the rent levels of exempt units as well as those that are directly regulated.

The second alternative would be to apply the relationship that exists today between the characteristics of rental housing units in the suburbs and their rent levels. However, suburban housing units and the suburban renter population are quite different from those of the District of Columbia. This makes it hard to accept an argument that, in the absence of controls, the relationships between unit characteristics and rents in the District would follow the patterns observed in the surrounding suburban jurisdictions.

Finally, the third approach would be to apply the relationships between housing characteristics and rent levels that existed in D.C. before the implementation of controls, and to look to other metropolitan areas for estimates of how central city rent levels have changed over the intervening years. This approach is by no means perfect, since metro-politan housing markets are all different. However, it is the best methodology available for our purposes. The 1974 American Housing Survey (AHS) for D.C. households is used to determine the contribution of various housing attributes to total rent in an unregulated market environment. Appendix D provides the results of a regression model expressing rents as a function of housing unit characteristics. This model has been used to estimate what today's units would have rented for in 1974--before the imposition of rent control.[1]

Once we have estimated the relationship that prevailed between housing unit characteristics and rent levels before the imposition of controls, the task still remains to determine how rapidly D.C. rent levels would have increased over the intervening years in the absence of the rent control program. During the 1970s and early 1980s, rent levels in D.C. grew more slowly than in most other central cities. Moreover, the District is unusual in that rents in the central city grew more slowly than in the surrounding suburbs during the 1970s and 1980s.

Table 5.1 presents the average annual rate of growth in median rents for the central cities and suburbs of several metropolitan areas in the Northeast and Middle-Atlantic regions. Two of these cities in addition to the District are rent controlled--Boston and Newark. They are included in table 5.1 for reference, but we obviously have not used them in the assessment of how D.C. rents would have changed in the absence of controls. Only one uncontrolled central city in the comparison set--Hartford--experienced a slower rate of rent inflation than its suburbs. On average, central city rent inflation exceeded suburban inflation by 0.55 percentage points annually.[2] From this we infer that, in the absence of controls, rents in D.C. would also have increased faster than in the surrounding suburbs.

At a minimum, we estimate that average rents in the District would have increased at a rate of about 8.8 percent annually--half a percentage point higher than the rate for the surrounding suburbs. In other words, in the absence of controls, the relationship between rent inflation in the District and its suburbs would have been more typical of other metropolitan areas. However, given the rates of rent inflation that prevailed in other central cities over the period, we consider it more likely that rents would have increased faster--at a rate of 9.5 percent annually. This "best estimate" of 9.5 percent annual rent inflation corresponds to the average rate experienced by the uncontrolled central cities listed in table 5.1, and by U.S. central cities generally.

Finally, given the above-average rate of income growth that occurred among D.C. renters in the 1970s and 1980s, it is possible that in the absence of controls, the pressure on rents would have been considerably higher here than in the comparison cities. As shown in table 5.1, median rent levels consistently increased at a faster pace than the median incomes among renter households in both central cities and suburban jurisdictions. In fact, among the uncontrolled central cities listed in the table, the annual rate of rent inflation averaged about four percentage points higher than the average annual rate of income growth among renter households. If the District had experienced this pattern in the absence of controls, rents would have increased by as much as 11 percent annually.

The task of estimating what rents would have been in the absence of controls is fraught with uncertainty. There is no unimpeachable source of evidence. Using the best available method, we estimate that, in the absence of controls, average rent levels would be significantly higher than those that prevail today. Even given the lower-bound estimate of an 8.8 percent annual rate of rent inflation, rents in the District today would average about $50 more in an unregulated market. And at the upper-bound estimate, unregulated rents would exceed today's levels by more than $200 on average. Our best estimate of a 9.5 percent annual rate of rent inflation implies that, in the absence of controls, D.C. renters would be paying between $95 and $100 more per month in rent (including utilities) than they do today.

Table 5.1   D.C. AND OTHER METROPOLITAN AREAS: PATTERNS OF RENT INFLATION

	Average Annual Increase in Median Rents		Average Annual Increase in Median Incomes	
	Central City (%)	Suburbs (%)	City (%)	Suburbs (%)
U.S. Average	9.4	8.9	5.3	5.9
Atlanta	10.2	9.0	6.0	6.6
Baltimore	8.9	8.8	3.9	6.4
Hartford	9.0	9.3	6.9	6.6
Philadelphia	9.9	7.7	5.3	5.5
Pittsburgh	11.5	11.0	6.4	5.7
Rochester	7.5	7.5	5.4	5.5
Boston[a]	9.4	8.8	5.7	5.9
Newark[a]	7.0	7.8	3.2	5.8
Washington, D.C.[a]	7.8	8.3	6.1	6.5

Source: Published American Housing Survey volumes, 1981-83. Washington, D.C.: U.S. Bureau of the Census.

a. Rents in Boston, Newark, and Washington, D.C., are all subject to local controls.

IMPACTS OF RENT CONTROL ON HOUSING AFFORDABILITY

Without question, the rent savings generated by controls in the District moderate the problems of housing affordability faced by D.C. renters. As figure 5.1 shows, at our "best estimates" of uncontrolled market rent levels, the share of households paying more than 30 percent of their income for rent would increase from its current level of about 43 percent to more than 50 percent.[3] Thus, while affordability problems in the District are severe today, a much larger number of renter households would pay excessive rent burdens in the absence of rent control. In fact, the median rent burdens would be much more typical of other central cities in the U.S. at these estimated market rent levels.

However, the rent savings generated by controls are not evenly distributed among all D.C. renters. In fact, not all households would be paying more in an uncontrolled market than they do today. About one-quarter of all D.C. renters probably pay rents as high--and perhaps higher--than the "market" rents that would prevail in the absence of controls. And, among those who experience rent savings, about one-third pay rents that are within $100 of estimated market rents, another third pay between $100 and $200 less they would in the absence of controls, and the remaining third pay rents that are more than $200 below market rent levels.

The households who enjoy the greatest rent savings are those who have remained in their controlled units for several years. The vast majority of households who occupy controlled units and who have remained in their units for six or more years enjoy substantial rent savings, while roughly half of those who are recent movers pay rents as high, or higher, than they would in the absence of controls. Our estimates suggest that, when controlled rental units are vacated, landlords sometimes raise rents to levels *above* those that would prevail in the absence of controls, to compensate for the fact that, if the new tenant stays for more than a year or two, rents will be constrained from rising as rapidly as they would in the absence of controls. Thus, the turnover history of controlled units plays an important role in determining the

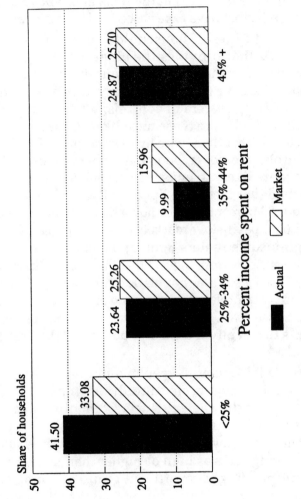

FIGURE 5.1 CONTROLLED AND EXEMPT RENTAL UNITS: RENT BURDENS WITH ACTUAL AND MARKET RENTS

Share of households

Percent income spent on rent

Actual   Market

Source: 1987 Urban Institute "Tenant Survey."

level of rent savings--with units that turn over frequently much more likely to charge rents at or above market levels than units that have experienced only occasional turnover.

What types of households benefit from a system of controls that provides the biggest savings to long-term stayers? In general, elderly households and families with children are the groups most likely to enjoy rent savings from the existing system of controls, while younger and more mobile singles are those most likely to pay rents that are as high or higher than those that would prevail in the absence of controls. Moreover, poor and moderate-income households are more likely to enjoy direct rent savings than are those with higher incomes. Specifically, as shown in figure 5.2, about 80 percent of poor households (annual incomes under $15,000) pay below-market rents, compared to 65 percent of high-income renters (annual incomes over $50,000). This pattern stems from the fact that the most affluent segments of the District's renter population consist of young singles and groups of unrelated adults, who are more likely to be recent movers and to occupy the newer, more expensive, and larger units that typify the exempt portion of the District's rental stock.

It is important to keep in mind that neither household composition nor income directly determines the level of rent savings under the existing system of rent control in the District of Columbia. An elderly couple or a low-income family who moved into their units this year would probably be paying rents as high or higher than market rents. And, correspondingly, an affluent group of young singles will begin to enjoy significant rent savings if they remain in a controlled unit for more than a year or two. The rent savings generated by controls are available to households of all types and income levels, but they arise primarily through the continuous occupancy of controlled units.

FIGURE 5.2 D.C. RENTAL UNITS:
ESTIMATED SHARE OF HOUSEHOLDS WITH
RENT SAVINGS, BY INCOME AND LIFE-CYCLE

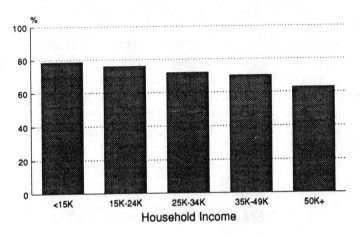

Household Income

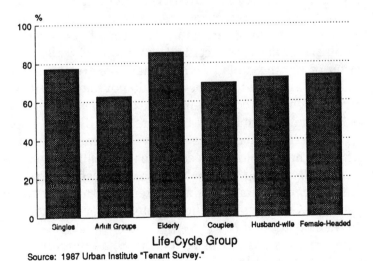

Life-Cycle Group

Source: 1987 Urban Institute "Tenant Survey."

The tendency for rent levels to be at or even above market levels for recently vacated units means that movers and newly forming households who are poor are especially likely to face unaffordable rent burdens. Because the existing system of controls is designed to generate benefits for those who remain in their units, poor households that are newly forming or mobile may actually have greater difficulty finding affordable housing than they would in an uncontrolled market. In fact, a large share of the poor households who stand at greatest risk of homelessness are recent movers whose rents are as high or higher than those that would prevail in the absence of rent control.

TENANT PERCEPTIONS AND CHOICE

District renters--including those living in both controlled and exempt units--strongly approve of rent control. For virtually all segments of the renter population, sentiment runs at least three to one in favor of rent control. Although D.C. renters are enthusiastic about rent control, many do not really know whether or not the units in which they live are controlled. Specifically, almost 40 percent either do not know or answer incorrectly when asked to identify the control status of their units.[4] Tenants in controlled units are more likely to know their control status than those who live in exempt units, and the share of households with accurate information increases systematically among those who have remained in the same units for several years. But the fact remains that two out of every five D.C. renters are either uninformed or misinformed about their status.

The primary benefit of rent control, as perceived by residents of controlled units, is that it makes rents more affordable. Roughly 90 percent of those who live in controlled rental units indicate that rent control has made their apartments more affordable. But tenants also value the sense of security provided by the existing system of controls; about 80 percent of those who live in controlled units say that rent control provides them with the security to stay in their apartments if they want to.[5] Most of these households (almost 75 percent) also indicate that rent control increases their incentive to stay in their existing apartments even if they might prefer to move. Thus, D.C. renters recognize that continuous occupancy of a controlled unit is what generates the greatest monetary savings under the existing system of controls, but this impediment to mobility does not appear to outweigh the benefits of controls in the minds of most.

Most tenants in controlled rental units (80 percent) believe that building maintenance is as good or better than it would be in the absence of rent controls, and a substantial share (61 percent) report that the protections offered by rent control make them more willing to insist on building repairs. Low-income households were particularly likely to include this as a benefit of the District's rent control program.

Although D.C. renters clearly realize that the benefits of the existing system of rent control increase with length of tenure, many appear to overestimate the monetary benefits they obtain. As figure 5.3 shows, almost three-quarters (73 percent) of D.C. renters believe that they would be paying higher rents in the absence of controls, and only 17 percent think that market rents would be the same or even lower than their current rents. In contrast, our estimates of market rents for D.C. units imply that about one-third of all renters would be paying roughly the same amount, or in some cases less, in the absence of controls. Recent movers are particularly likely to think they are obtaining direct rent savings, whereas our estimates suggest that they are paying as much or more than they would in the absence of controls.

Given its direct, monetary impacts, rent control might be expected to alter the behavior of D.C. renter households --discouraging them from moving even when an existing unit does not meet their needs, encouraging them to remain in the District rather than moving to the suburbs, or encouraging them to remain renters rather than becoming homeowners. After examining patterns of housing choice in D.C. and other central cities, we concluded that the District's existing system of rent control may contribute to the very low rate of mobility observed among D.C. renters, but it probably has not had any significant impact on homeownership rates or on the choice of central city versus suburban locations.

D.C. renters who live in controlled units move less frequently than those who occupy units that are exempt from controls. For example, half of all controlled units have been occupied by the same household for at least six years, compared to only about one-third of the District's exempt units. Moreover, D.C. renters are less mobile than renters in many other central cities; between 1980 and 1981, roughly 20 percent of D.C. renters moved, compared to 30 percent of all central city renters in the U.S.[6] However, as of 1981, there were other central cities with equally low mobility rates that did not have rent control--Baltimore and Philadelphia, for example. And mobility rates among D.C. renters were just as low, both in absolute terms and in comparison to other cities, before the imposition of rent control as they were in 1981, suggesting that, while controls may be a factor in mobility decisions here, they are not the only explanation for the low rate of turnover in the District's rental housing inventory.

Since 1981, mobility rates in D.C. have plummeted; today only about 10 percent of unsubsidized renters in D.C. report that they moved within the last year. Although a decade of experience with rent control may have contributed to the very low rate of household mobility, the declining availability of units that are affordable for households with low and mod-

FIGURE 5.3 D.C. RENTER PERCEPTIONS AND
URBAN INSTITUTE CALCULATIONS OF AMOUNT
RENT WOULD CHANGE WITHOUT RENT CONTROL

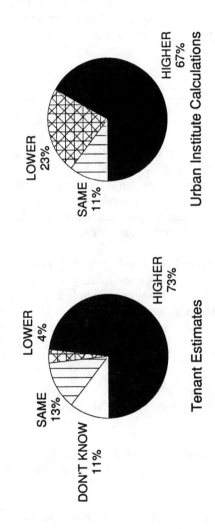

Source: Urban Institute "Tenant Survey."

erate incomes probably also discourages such households from moving. In other words, the District's rental housing market has become considerably tighter over the course of the 1980s, a trend that explains the heightened level of additions to the stock in recent years as well as the depressed rate of household mobility.

Notes, chapter five

1. It is important to note that this approach does not assume that the characteristics of D.C. rental units are the same today as in 1974 or that they would have been the same in the absence of controls. Instead, we assume that the *relative* costs of different types of units would have remained essentially the same over the last decade if rent controls had not been implemented.

2. We considered the possibility that these rates of rent inflation might reflect increases in the quality of central city housing as well as price inflation. We were not able to estimate constant quality measures of the rate of rent inflation for all of our comparison cities, but we did so for the District and its suburbs. In these jurisdictions, the constant quality rates of rent inflation correspond closely to increases in median rents.

3. Of course, the estimated impact of controls on the incidence of affordability problems varies with the estimated rate of market rent inflation.

4. For a subset of the households in our tenant survey, we were able to determine the actual control status from DCRA registration records.

5. Note that many D.C. renters--as well as landlords--do not distinguish the rent stabilization program from eviction protections. Thus, some of the benefits tenants attribute to rent control

actually stem from the District's accompanying system of eviction protections.

6. The comparatively low mobility rate observed for D.C. renters applies to all segments of the renter population except for the elderly. For example, in 1981 24 percent of nonelderly singles and 19 percent of poor renters in the District were recent movers, compared to 34 percent and 31 percent, respectively, for all U.S. cities. Among the elderly, roughly 9 percent moved annually, in D.C. and in U.S. central cities generally.

Chapter Six

IMPACTS OF RENT CONTROL:
THE LANDLORD'S PERSPECTIVE

Rent control cannot make rental housing more affordable without also making it less profitable as an investment opportunity. This chapter examines the financial data collected for controlled rental properties in the District and in our survey of owners and managers of controlled properties to assess the impacts of the District's rent control program on profitability and on investment in the rental stock.

IMPACTS OF CONTROLS ON PROFITABILITY

Given our estimate that rent control reduces gross rent levels (rents plus utilities) by an average of $95 to $100 per month, rent revenues to D.C. landlords are obviously also reduced. In the absence of controls, our estimates of prevailing "market" rents for controlled units would yield substantially higher gross revenues--about 33 percent higher on average.[1]

The increased rent revenues that would prevail in the absence of controls would ultimately increase property values as well, so that the impacts of controls on the returns to investment in rental property are more complex than they may at first appear. We assumed that the ratio of rent revenues to assessed property values that prevails today would be essentially the same in the absence of controls. Thus, higher revenues translate directly into higher value estimates. We also assumed that loan- to value-ratios would be roughly the same, so that both equity and debt would increase if values were higher. Finally, our estimates of appreciation benefits in the absence of controls assume no change in appreciation *rates*, but apply the prevailing rates to the estimated values of properties in the absence of controls. Details of these calculations are presented in appendix E.

Based on these assumptions, table 6.1 summarizes the estimated impacts of rent control on key financial attributes for average units in different building size categories. After adjusting for changes in equity, interest costs, and property taxes, we estimate that D.C. landlords would realize annual increases in net income ranging from about $600 per unit in small properties to about $1,350 per unit in large controlled properties. At the same time, annual appreciation gains would probably grow by amounts ranging from just over $100 per unit in large properties to $800 per unit in the smallest properties.

If these increased revenues were entirely devoted to raising the investment returns to D.C. landlords, the profitability of the average large rental property would rise by as much as five percentage points, while the profitability of smaller properties would rise by only one or two percentage points. But the majority of controlled housing providers in the District stated that, if their revenues were to rise significantly, either maintenance expenditures would be increased or property improvements would be undertaken, as indicated by responses to the following survey question:

"If your property experienced a significant increase in revenues, this increase would be used to ..."	*Responses (%)*
Increase returns to investors	37.5
Undertake deferred maintenance or capital improvements	66.7
Enhance routine maintenance	23.1

Table 6.1   AVERAGE ANNUAL AFTER-TAX RETURNS WITH
              AND WITHOUT RENT CONTROL, 1985

	Actual (%)	Estimated Market (%)
1- to 2-unit buildings	10.4	11.3
3- to 4-unit buildings	18.7	20.5
5- to 9-unit buildings	12.4	14.2
10- to 19-unit buildings	11.7	14.6
20- to 49-unit buildings	10.3	13.9
50- to 99-unit buildings	11.8	14.3
100- to 249-unit buildings	12.4	15.8
250+-unit buildings	10.1	15.1

If the typical housing provider used half of the increase in net operating revenues to either expand maintenance or finance property improvements, then the estimated profitability of the average large rental property would increase by about two percentage points, while the profitability of small properties would increase by less than one percentage point on average.

Although profits would probably be higher in the absence of controls, during the 1980s the District's automatic rent adjustment mechanism generally kept pace with increases in operating costs. As illustrated in figure 6.1, even for units continuously occupied from 1981 through 1987, allowable rent adjustments met or exceeded increases in the costs of operations for most types of rental properties.[2] Specifically, the increase of general applicability resulted in a cumulative increase of 31 percent in rent levels over the 1981-87 period. Average properties in most size categories experienced cumulative operating cost increases at or below this level.

Only properties in the three- to four-unit size category experienced substantially higher increases--averaging about 41 percent. Our analysis suggests that the above-average rate of cost escalation experienced by these properties was primarily attributable to dramatic increases in assessed values and, therefore, to property taxes and interest payments. Thus, these properties have experienced above-average cost increases and reduced cash flow over the past several years, but their property values, and, hence, appreciation benefits, have increased substantially as well.

IMPACTS ON THE HOUSING STOCK

There is conflicting evidence regarding the impacts of rent control on the maintenance of rental housing in the District. On the one hand, rent revenues would be 33 percent higher on average in the absence of controls and, as outlined earlier, these increased revenues would yield sizable annual increases in net operating incomes. According to D.C. housing providers, the increases estimated for average units would be sufficient to correct deferred maintenance problems for roughly half of the units that are currently in less-than-adequate physical condition. Moreover, among providers who reported that their units were in deteriorated physical condition or that current levels of maintenance expenditures were not sufficient to preserve the quality of their properties, insufficient revenue was the most frequent--although not the only--explanation, as shown by responses to the following query:

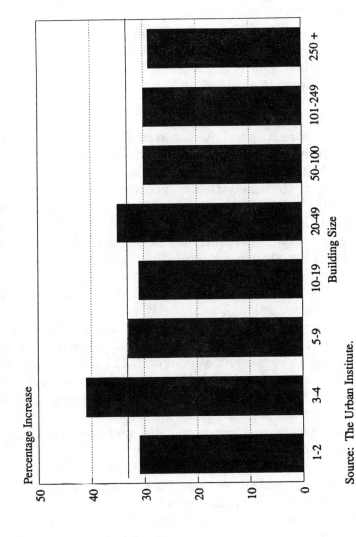

FIGURE 6.1 PERCENTAGE OPERATING COST
INCREASE BY BUILDING SIZE, IN D.C., 1981

Percentage Increase

Building Size

Source: The Urban Institute.

For properties in less than adequate condition, reasons for not undertaking needed repairs--	*Responses (%)*
Rent revenues are not high enough.	87.3
Neighborhood conditions.	31.4
Cannot obtain financing.	7.8
Building is occupied.	5.6

Thus, there are good reasons to conclude that, in the absence of controls, at least a portion of the increased rent revenues would be used for property maintenance and improvements, and that the amounts involved would probably be large enough to have a significant impact on property conditions. If housing providers devoted incremental rent revenues to housing repairs and improved maintenance, the quality of the rental housing stock would be better in the absence of controls.

However, there is no indication that a decade and a half of local rent control has actually resulted in the physical deterioration of D.C. rental housing. Since 1974, the share of physically deficient units has actually declined--from 26 percent to 20 percent. Moreover, D.C. units that are exempt from controls exhibit a higher rate of deficiencies than those subject to controls (25 percent versus 20 percent), despite the fact that uncontrolled units are typically more expensive.[3] Finally, tenants in our survey did not believe that landlords were neglecting housing maintenance as a result of rent control, and, in fact, many indicated that the existing system of controls made them more confident about asking landlords to correct physical deficiencies in their units.

Since rent control significantly reduces rent revenues for the majority of D.C. units, some providers may be discouraged from adding new or rehabilitated units to the rental inventory, and others may remove units from the available supply. Moreover, even if investment in D.C. rental property is reasonably profitable, some members of the real estate industry argue that the existing climate of vigorous tenant protection--including rent control, housing code enforcement, eviction protections, and condominium conversion restrictions--is sufficiently costly and intimidating to discourage investment within the District of Columbia.

Landlords report that they perceive the District's regulatory environment as having major impacts on their operations. Owners of virtually all controlled units in our sample expressed the belief that rent control has a major impact on their revenues, and a majority also viewed the administrative costs of rent control as a significant factor in their operations, as shown by the following survey:

D.C. Regulations Perceived to Have a Major Impact On:	Percentage of Controlled Units
Revenues	90
Administrative costs	84
Eviction costs and delays	77
Property value	50
Unit recovery	30
Substantial rehabilitation decisions	24

Moreover, owners of 80 percent of controlled rental units in D.C. indicated that they did not expect to invest in D.C. rental housing in the future. The reasons most commonly cited were that rents were not high enough to make rental real estate an attractive investment (45.5 percent), and that the

D.C. regulatory environment makes investment in other jurisdictions more attractive (50.2 percent).[4] It is interesting to note, however, that among small individual owners, the most common reason given for avoiding future investment was not the local regulatory environment but the expectation that the new federal tax law will make rental real estate a less attractive investment than it has been in the past.

Do recent trends in the size of the District's rental stock support the argument that rent control reduces housing supply? The precipitous decline in the size of the District's rental housing stock that occurred during the 1970s and early 1980s is often cited as evidence that rent control chokes off supply. Rent control and the other tenant protections that accompany it may have been an important factor in the decisions of some potential investors. In particular, rent control may have discouraged owners of single-family homes, who could easily sell their units on the burgeoning home-ownership market, from keeping these houses in the rental inventory. However, evidence of comparable stock losses in other, uncontrolled central cities over the same period strongly suggests that the local regulatory environ-ment should not be blamed for the current shortage of low- and moderate-cost rental housing in the District.

The 1970s was a period in which many U.S. central cities--controlled as well as uncontrolled--experienced declining rental housing inventories. As discussed earlier, this decline was triggered not by local regulatory conditions but by nationwide economic trends that made home-ownership overwhelmingly attractive; by the expansion of suburban housing opportunities; and by the declining purchasing power of the households who continued to rely on the rental market (see accompanying data for seven central cities).

Average Annual Percent Change
in Rental Inventory, 1970-83:

Atlanta	-0.4
Baltimore	-0.9
Hartford	-1.4
Philadelphia	-0.4
Pittsburgh	-1.4
Rochester	-0.8
Washington, D.C.	-1.4

Units were withdrawn from central city rental inventories, and the level of new (unsubsidized) rental production was low because fewer middle- and high-income households were choosing to be central city renters, and because the remaining renters could not afford to make housing investment sufficiently profitable.

Even during the 1970s, when the rental stock was shrinking, new rental units were being built in the District. In fact, D.C. experienced a higher rate of new rental housing construction than many uncontrolled cities, as shown by the following:

Average Annual Rate of New
Rental Construction, 1973-80 (%):

Atlanta	2.0
Baltimore	1.8
Hartford	0.0
Philadelphia	0.7
Pittsburgh	0.0
Rochester	2.0
Washington, D.C.	1.5

Between 1970 and 1981, while the District's rental housing inventory experienced a net loss of more than 1,000 units annually on average, roughly 400 new rental units were built each year. While about three-quarters of these new units received federal subsidy assistance, other, uncontrolled central cities in the Northeast and Middle-Atlantic regions experienced much lower rates of new rental construction during the 1970s.

During the first half of the 1980s, the decline in demand for rental housing in the District slowed considerably. Specifically, between 1974 and 1981, the number of renter households in the District fell by almost 3,000 per year on average. Between 1981 and 1985, this annual figure fell to below 1,000. In other words, demand for rental housing in the District began to stabilize during the first half of the 1980s, in part because rising interest rates, lower inflation, and reductions in marginal tax rates have all contributed to make homeownership much less affordable relative to rental housing. In fact, the rate of homeownership in the nation as a whole, which increased from 64.2 percent to 65.6 percent in the 1970s, declined to 64.0 percent by 1987, with affluent singles and childless couples as well as young families electing to continue renting rather than entering the home-ownership market.

However, although the loss of renter households slowed considerably during the 1980s, the supply of rental units continued its decline at a somewhat faster pace. The result was a dramatic drop in the rental vacancy rate from 6.2 percent in 1981 to 2.5 percent in 1985. More recently, the District's rental stock has started to grow in size, increasing by about 800 units annually since 1985. In part, this turnaround reflects the conversion and sale restrictions enacted in 1981, which sharply limit the circumstances in which rental properties can be converted to owner-occupancy or otherwise removed from the inventory. But, in addition, the resurgence of demand for rental housing--reflected in falling vacancy rates--appears to have attracted new invest-ment in the District's rental housing market. In other words, the recent increase in the size of the rental inventory represents a lagged market response to renewed levels of effective demand.

It is possible that this response might have occurred more quickly in an unregulated rental market, but the responsiveness of District investors to the changing demands for rental housing--and the similarity of recent trends in uncontrolled central city markets--suggests that rent control is not a determining factor in investment decisionmaking, although it certainly may be a consideration. Recent investors in new and substantially rehabilitated rental units reported that they do not see rent control as a deterrent, and only about one-quarter of those interviewed advocated the elimination of rent control. More cited the District's system of eviction protections--which is seen to reflect a strong "pro-tenant" bias in the local regulatory environment--as a serious cause for concern. In addition, the cost and availability of land and/or structures for new construction and substantial rehabilitation, as well as the availability of long-term financing, were cited by the owners of new rental properties as critical constraints on their ability to build or substantially renovate housing in the District.[5]

Although additions to the rental housing stock do not appear to be very sensitive to the presence of rent control, losses from the rental stock actually have a much greater impact on the availability of housing for low- and moderate-income renters. And over the last decade and a half, rental inventory losses have been much more volatile than inventory additions. During the 1970s, an average of 1,000 units were removed from the District's housing stock annually, and the vast majority of these units rented for less than $350 (1987 dollars). Again, this phenomenon was by no means unique to

the District; many uncontrolled central cities also lost rental
units during the 1970s:

Annual Rate of Rental
Unit Removals, 1973-80 (%):

Atlanta	2.7
Baltimore	3.0
Hartford	4.4
Philadelphia	3.2
Pittsburgh	4.0
Rochester	5.3
Washington, D.C.	4.5

These losses reflect the overall decline in demand for central
city rental housing relative to homeownership as well as to
suburban housing opportunities.

Another important explanation for the removal of units
from the rental inventory is the declining purchasing power
of low-income renter households. Increasingly, the amounts
that low- and moderate-income renters can afford to pay for
housing fall short of what it costs to provide decent rental
accommodations. Thus, as rental units age, they are more
likely to drop out of the inventory altogether than to filter
down to form a stock of older but decent and affordable
rental housing.

Rent control has not caused this problem, but it may play
a contributing role in the removal of units from the District's
rental housing stock. Our inventory of additions to and
losses from the District's rental housing inventory indicates
that roughly 160 rental units were either temporarily or
permanently removed from housing use between May 1985
and April 1987. Almost all of these units were controlled, and
owners who were interviewed consistently listed rent control

among the negative factors that caused them to discontinue the use of their properties. Their decisions were motivated by the lack of economic viability of their properties, and they suggested that if the District government wants to minimize losses from the rental stock, it should both make it easier to evict nonpaying and destructive tenants, and approve legitimate substantial rehabilitation and hardship petitions more readily.

In principle, the substantial rehabilitation and hardship petition provisions of the District's existing system of rent control should address the problems of properties that are financially and physically distressed. In fact, even though properties of this kind may be technically eligible for a hardship rent increase, their tenants may not be able to afford substantially higher rents, even if they were approved. As a result, many of these properties are likely to deteriorate further, and ultimately may be removed from the rental inventory--directly reducing the availability of housing for low- and moderate-income renters.

Rent control clearly plays a role in this scenario, but as a complicating factor, rather than a primary cause. If rent control alone constrained the rents that the landlords of distressed properties could charge, and if market rents for these units were sufficiently high to induce landlords to improve them in the absence of controls, then we would certainly observe a much higher usage of the hardship petition process, despite the costs. Given the relatively low usage of substantial rehabilitation, capital improvements, and hardship petition opportunities, it is hard to argue that rent control, per se, is the binding constraint on the economic viability of these properties.

Notes, chapter six

1. From the perspective of tenants (including those living in both controlled and exempt units), the estimated rents that would prevail in the absence of controls would increase housing expenditures by $95 to $100 per month on average. The same market rent estimates yield a 33 percent increase in "contract" rents for controlled properties on average. Contract rents exclude utilities that are paid directly by tenants.

2. Our estimates of the rate of actual operating cost inflation in the District are based on price changes for each operating cost item. See appendix F for details.

3. Part of the explanation for this result may be that a large share of exempt units is composed of single-family homes, which are not subject to housing code inspections except on a complaint basis.

4. Note that respondents could select more than one primary reason why future investment was not planned.

5. Because the number of providers who have added units to the stock between 1985 and 1987 and who could be reached for telephone interviews was small (17 interviews), we cannot provide statistical breakdowns of their responses.

Chapter Seven

CONCLUSIONS

Advocates often advance rent control as a panacea for problems of housing affordability, while opponents blame controls for the poor quality and dwindling supply of low-cost units. In the District of Columbia, neither of these extreme positions is supported by the facts. Rent control appears to have moderated the housing affordability problem, but has by no means solved it. And there is no convincing evidence that controls have significantly deterred investment in either maintenance or new construction, although the profitability of rental housing would be higher in the absence of controls.

Economic theory suggests that, certainly over the long term, any substantial price effect (reduced rents) must yield a supply effect (lower quality or fewer units). As a result, most economic analyses argue that the benefits of rent control--more affordable rent levels--are ultimately outweighed by the costs--deferred maintenance and limited availability of units. Our evidence, however, suggests that rent control in the District of Columbia has had little or no supply effect, despite over a decade of moderated rent increases. How, then, can these empirical results be explained in the context of conventional models of the workings of a reasonably competitive market for rental housing?

First, it is important to recapitulate four key features of the District's system of rent control:

- New and substantially rehabilitated rental projects are exempt from controls;

- In controlled properties, rents can increase every year;

- Landlords who improve controlled properties can apply for rent adjustments to cover the costs of these improvements; and

- If a controlled property is in financial distress, the owner can apply for a hardship rent adjustment, to bring the annual cash return up to 12 percent of current equity in the project.

Like other rent control programs implemented in U.S. cities during the 1970s, the District's system provides incentives for landlords to maintain their existing rental properties and to produce new ones. Investors who add to the supply of rental housing are not subject to regulatory restrictions on the rents they charge. And landlords who maintain controlled properties adequately can automatically increase rents each year. In addition to this automatic rent adjustment mechanism, landlords in the District can petition for rent increases to cover property improvements or to correct conditions of financial hardship.

Thus, the District's rent control regime is a moderate one that explicitly seeks to maintain the profitability of investment in rental housing. In fact, while rent revenues and investor profits would have been higher in the absence of controls, after-tax profit levels for rental housing in the District are competitive with alternative investment opportunities. And, over the period since the imposition of rent controls, the quality of the District's rental stock has not deteriorated. Moreover, although the number of units available for rent declined over much of the period that rent control has been in effect, this decline is comparable to that experienced in many other cities, and is largely attributable to a drop off in the level of demand for rental housing in the District.

It is possible that the reason rent control has had no impact on supply is that its impact on price has been negligible. In other words, perhaps the District's system of regulation has been so moderate that rents today are within $50 of the levels that would have prevailed in the absence of controls. We obviously cannot know for certain what rents would have been in an unregulated market. But evidence from other metropolitan housing markets around the U.S. strongly suggests that the District's rent control program has moderated rent levels by at least $50 per month on average, if not more.

If so, then in the absence of controls, landlords would have earned--and in other rental markets did earn--excessive profits. How can landlords earn excessive profits over the long term without either losing tenants to more competitive landlords, or attracting new investors in search of high profits? In a competitive market, one could argue, rent control should either be counterproductive or irrelevant. However, there are a number of imperfections in the market for rental housing that--in the absence of regulation--might allow investors to earn excess profits over an extended period, and that therefore may make rent control a legitimate public sector intervention.

Imperfect Information. The nature of housing services per se makes it difficult for tenants to "shop around" on a regular basis for the best price-quantity combinations. More specifically, the supply of rental housing is extremely diverse in terms of unit attributes, services, and location. This makes it difficult for renters to compare one unit and its price to the competition. Finding out about alternative rental units and their prices is a time-consuming process that households are not likely to undertake unless they are seriously contemplating a move.

High Transactions Costs. Moving is expensive--both financially and psychically. This discourages households from shopping around regularly for the best deals in rental housing, and contributes to the lack of information about competing units and their rent levels. Moreover, even in the absence of controls, landlords typically offer their long-term stayers a tenure discount. In other words, even a landlord who is earning excess profits probably charges his staying tenants less than a competing landlord charges newcomers, because turnover is expensive for the landlord as well as for the tenant. This means that tenants save money in the short run by staying in their existing units, even if a competing unit might be cheaper in the long run.

Segmented Market. The existing rental stock is highly segmented--on the basis of unit size, amenities, physical quality, location, and price. If there is a limited supply of units in some segments of the market, then in the absence of controls, owners of these units can raise rents rapidly without worrying about losing tenants.

High Entry Costs. It is substantially more expensive to build new units than to maintain existing units. As a result, competition from new and substantially rehabilitated housing is not an effective constraint on rent levels for existing units. Moreover, since new construction will of necessity be designed to serve the most affluent segments of the renter population (primarily young singles in D.C.), it will not create competition for the segments of the stock that serve poorer renters (primarily families). It is conceivable that very high rents (and profits) in large units would generate incentives to convert owner-occupied homes to rental use. However, during the 1970s, homeownership pressures were so intense that house values rose too rapidly to make single-family homes very attractive as competitively priced rental properties.

Barriers to Entry. Limited availability and high costs of developable land in the central city discourage investors from building new units, except when there is clear evidence of very high demand among affluent renters. In fact, owners of new rental housing in the District were much more likely to cite land availability and costs as barriers to development than the effects of rent control.

Low- and moderate-income households in the District of Columbia face a serious shortage of rental housing that they can afford. Regulating rent increases has been at least partially successful in moderating the problem of housing affordability, but it has by no means eliminated the problem of excessive housing cost burdens. Although many of the households who benefit from rent control have low and moderate incomes, others are quite affluent. And by targeting relief primarily to renters who remain in their units for several years, the District's system provides no assistance to frequent movers or to newly forming households. No system of rent control can ensure the availability of decent and affordable housing for low- and moderate-income renters. Whether or not cities regulate rents' more direct remedies are clearly required, including programs that supplement the rents that low- and moderate-income tenants can afford to pay, that preserve existing low-rent properties, and that induce the production of additional low- and moderate-cost rental units.

APPENDICES

Appendix A

THE URBAN INSTITUTE'S STUDY OF RENT CONTROL IN THE DISTRICT OF COLUMBIA

In March 1987, the District of Columbia's Department of Consumer and Regulatory Affairs (DCRA) contracted with The Urban Institute to conduct a study of rent control in the District. This study, which was completed in October 1988, was mandated by Section 220 of the Rental Housing Act of 1985 (D.C. Law 6-10). Its purpose was to provide a factual basis for determining the continued need for rent stabilization in Washington, D.C.

The overall content of the study was defined by nine specific items delineated by the City Council:

1. The number of new or renovated units placed on the District's rental market after May 1, 1985.

2. The number of new or renovated units projected to be placed on the District's rental market through 1996.

3. An assessment of the effectiveness of the Tenant Assistance Program (TAP) and the projected cost of TAP in the absence of rent control.

4. The impact of rent control on the cost and supply of rental housing.

5. An assessment of the present rent control program in terms of its ability to be understood, and its efficiency, economy, equity, and flexibility.

6. The impact of rent control on small housing providers.

7. The number of District residents living in substandard housing and their location.

8. An assessment of the impact of the Civil Infractions Act on the enforcement of the District's housing code regulations.

9. An assessment of the impact on both the rental housing market and the rent stabilization program of vacancy decontrol, luxury decontrol, increasing the small landlord exemption from 4 to 10 rental units, and using the percentage of family income available for rent as a component of a rent control formula.

To effectively address the City Council's mandate to conduct a comprehensive analysis of the impacts of rent control in the District of Columbia, The Urban Institute compiled an extensive database, including up-to-date information about renter households and their housing circumstances, housing providers and the physical and financial condition of their properties, stock losses and additions, and the operation of the rent control program, housing code enforcement, and the Tenant Assistance Program. Existing data compiled by city agencies and by the U.S. Census provided a starting point, but the overall analysis relied on eight major sources, all but one of which constitute new data collected specifically for this effort:

- The American Housing Survey (AHS). The U.S. Bureau of the Census conducts regular surveys of households and housing units for 59 metropolitan areas, including the District of Columbia and its suburbs. Our analysis makes extensive use of the 1974 AHS data for the Washington, D.C., metropolitan area, as well as key indicators for 1977 and 1981. The AHS was most recently conducted in the D.C. metropolitan area in 1985, and we have obtained counts of rental households and housing units from this survey. However, since the 1985 AHS was not released by the Census until the end of the study period, we were not able to analyze individual household observations. Finally, we refer at numerous points throughout this report to published AHS data for other central cities--with and without rent control--in the Northeast and Middle-Atlantic states.

- 1987 survey of renter households. During the summer of 1987, The Urban Institute, with the help of Lawrence Johnson and Associates, conducted telephone interviews with 3,000 D.C. renters and 600 renters in nearby suburban jurisdictions. These interviews provided data on household characteristics, housing conditions, rent levels, and attitudes toward the rent control program. Household responses regarding the control status of their units were verified against data in DCRA registration files.

- Financial statements for controlled properties. For a sample of 814 controlled rental properties, 1985 financial statements were collected from DCRA registration files. These financial statements were verified by comparing summary tabulations of income and expense items with tabulations of the D.C. Department of Finance and Revenue (DFR) data for the same properties. Confidentiality restrictions prevented The Urban Institute from obtaining direct access to DFR financial data for individual properties.

- 1987 survey of D.C. housing providers. The owners and/or managers of the 814 controlled rental properties for which financial statements were obtained were asked to provide additional factual and attitudinal data on a mail-back questionnaire. Providers of a representative sample of 244 controlled rental properties respond-ed to this questionnaire.

- Inventory of stock losses and additions. Drawing from D.C. Certificates of Occupancy, Tenant Eviction Petitions, and Condominium Conversion Registrations, The Urban Institute constructed an inventory of all additions to and losses from the District's rental housing stock from May 1, 1985, through April 30, 1987. In addition, telephone interviews were conducted with the housing providers responsible for a subset of these additions and losses.

- Housing code enforcement histories. For a subsample of 319 controlled rental properties, a year's history of housing code enforcement activity was recorded from the records of DCRA's Housing Inspections Division.

- Rent control petitions records. The volume and case-by-case disposition of 1985-87 housing provider and tenant petitions were gathered from DCRA records.

- Tenant Assistance Program participation. Staff of ICF, a subcontractor to The Urban Institute, collected and coded data on a representative sample of TAP applicants and program participants as of January 1988.

Information provided by these structured and objective data sources was supplemented by numerous personal interviews conducted with tenant advocates, housing providers, developers, and public officials. In these interviews, Urban Institute research staff members sought to understand the subjective perspectives of key actors in the D.C. rental housing market and to interpret the implications of the study's empirical results.

The D.C. rent control study culminated in a two-volume final report, which addresses all of the original nine study items and documents the data sources and analytical methods. The first volume presents the study findings for nontechnical readers and is titled, *Rent Control and the Availability of Affordable Housing in the District of Columbia: A Delicate Balance,* October 1988. The second volume consists of nine, independent technical reports, detailing methods and findings from the various components of the study. It is titled *Rent Control in the District of Columbia: Technical Supplement,* October 1988.

Urban Institute staff members who played major roles in the collection and analysis of data for the study and in the preparation of report sections include: G. Thomas Kingsley, Project Director, Margery Austin Turner, Principle Researcher; Marcia Carroll; Amina H.N. Elmi; Kathleen G. Heintz;

Barbara J. Lipman; Martha K. Nicholson; Douglas B. Page; Makiko Ueno; and J. Christopher Walker.

SURVEYS, SAMPLES, AND ANALYTIC METHODS

1987 URBAN INSTITUTE SURVEY OF D.C. AND SUBURBAN RENTERS

During the summer of 1987, The Urban Institute--with the assistance of Lawrence Johnson and Associates (LJA) --surveyed a sample of renter households in the District of Columbia and the surrounding suburban jurisdictions.

Sampling and Survey Procedures

Sampling and survey procedures were designed to produce a random sample of 3,000 unsubsidized D.C. renter house- holds. The basis for the sample was a random dialing technique employed in three portions of Virginia within the Capital Beltway. For each of these three areas, unique telephone numbers were selected for inclusion in the sample by systematically drawing from all working blocks of numbers in all telephone exchanges assigned to the area. (A working block is defined as 100 contiguous telephone numbers containing three or more residential telephone listings.)

The sample of telephone numbers included 17,316 D.C. telephone numbers and 2,727 telephone numbers for each of Maryland and Virginia. These large sample sizes were established to ensure that 3,000 D.C. surveys and 600 suburban surveys were ultimately completed. For each of the three areas, the total sample was divided into several sample replicates, to ensure that the ultimate sample of respondents was representative of the original sample of telephone numbers.

For each telephone number dialed, several questions were asked at the outset of the interview to determine whether the respondent was an unsubsidized renter household. If not, the interview was terminated. Due to the combination of unanswered telephones, nonworking numbers, nonresidential, owner-occupant or subsidized respondents, and unwillingness to participate in the survey, the rate of completions was fairly low. Nevertheless, the target of 3,000 D.C. interviews and 300 interviews each in Maryland and Virginia was achieved.

The survey was administered by Lawrence Johnson and Associates, using a Computer Assisted Telephone Interviewing (CATI) system. This system computerized the questionnaire itself, as well as a list of telephone numbers to call, records of previous attempts to reach sample numbers, and questionnaire responses. The CATI system was designed to prevent some of the most common interviewer errors, such as failure to follow skip patterns, and to detect illogical responses. Usually, errors of this kind have to be detected and corrected after data collection; the CATI system avoids many errors by only prompting the interviewer to ask questions that are relevant based on responses to earlier questions, and by making range and logic checks during the process of data collection. In addition, since interviewers enter responses to the survey directly into the computer as the interview is conducted, potential transcription errors are minimized.

Interviewers were supervised at all times. To ensure that questions were being asked correctly, supervisors monitored a sample of the telephone interviews. In addition, supervisors reinterviewed a sample of each day's completed interviews. In these verification interviews, the supervisor asked whether anyone in the household had been interviewed about their housing, and reasked three simple short-answer items to confirm that the interview had in fact been completed.

When an interviewer encountered a respondent who did not speak English and who could not bring an English-speaking person to the telephone, a written record was made of the telephone number. This number was then temporarily removed from the automated dialing list, with a notation regarding the language that the respondent seemed to be speaking. When several such cases accumulated, an interviewer with appropriate language skills was called to administer the questionnaires. Specifically, Spanish- and Vietnamese-speaking interviewers were available to conduct interviews. Respondents who could not understand these interviewers were dropped from the sample.

Consideration was given to administering a separate survey to a sample of households without telephones. This strategy was implemented in The Urban Institute's study of rent control in Los Angeles, on the assumption that poor households are the most likely to lack telephones, and that the responses of households without telephones may be systematically different from those of households with telephones. In Los Angeles, however, we found that the inclusion of the nontelephone respondents in the household survey had no impact on the distribution of responses. Moreover, as discussed later in this appendix, the Institute's survey obtained a more-than-adequate number of responses from poor households. Therefore, we concluded that a survey of nontelephone households was unnecessary.

Sample Characteristics

The sampling and survey procedures produced a sample of 3,000 D.C. interviews that closely represents the unsubsidized D.C. renter population. Nevertheless, we found that the representativeness of the D.C. sample could be improved by reweighting. The suburban samples were not reweighted because they were small and because their use was primarily for comparison purposes.

The raw data in D.C. overrepresent affluent households at the expense of low- and middle-income renters. The first two panels in table B.1 compare the distribution of households in our D.C. sample to the distribution of D.C. renter households in the 1981 American Housing Survey (AHS). Subsidized households--who are excluded from our sample--have been deleted from the AHS income distribution, but not from the other AHS distributions shown in this table. In addition, 1981 income ranges have been updated to 1987 dollars, using the D.C. all-item consumer price index.

Since it seems unlikely that the distribution of renter households by broad income category changed significantly from 1981 to 1987, we concluded that our sample includes too many affluent households, and not enough moderate- and middle-income households. Nevertheless, our sample includes sufficient numbers of responses in each income range to yield reliable results. We hypothesize that the over-representation of high-income renters may explain the apparent overrepresentation of college graduates, the slight underrepresentation of large households, and, possibly, the overrepresentation of efficiency units. Nevertheless, the distribution of 1987 survey respondents corresponds reasonably well to the distribution of AHS households on most household and dwelling unit characteristics.

The deviation between our sample and the distribution of unsubsidized renter households reported in AHS is large

Table B.1   COMPARISON OF 1981 AHS AND 1987
             URBAN INSTITUTE SAMPLES

	1981 AHS/(%)		1987 Survey Raw Data/(%)		Weighted Data/(%)	
Household Characteristics						
Income						
< $15,00	54,400	(38.9)	903	(32.4)	1,085	(38.9)
$15,000-$25,000	39,300	(28.1)	784	(28.1)	784	(28.1)
$25,000-$35,000	30,400	(21.7)	463	(16.6)	606	(21.7)
$35,000-$50,000	7,400	(5.3)	297	(10.6)	148	(5.3)
$50,000+	8,300	(5.9)	342	(12.3)	166	(5.9)
Education						
No high school diploma	21,400	(13.4)	314	(10.5)	307	(11.1)
High school	72,000	(45.0)	885	(29.7)	877	(31.7)
Some college	23,600	(14.8)	655	(22.0)	614	(22.2)
College graduate	42,900	(26.8)	1,123	(37.7)	968	(35.0)
Household Size						
One person	72,100	(45.1)	1,334	(44.9)	1,284	(47.0)
2 people	41,300	(25.8)	873	(29.4)	776	(28.4)
3-4 people	33,900	(21.2)	613	(20.6)	536	(19.6)
5+ people	12,500	(7.8)	153	(5.1)	134	(4.9)
Dwelling Unit Characteristics						
Year Structure Built						
Since 1981	N/A	--	31	(2.8)	26	(2.4)
1970-81	7,800	(4.9)	69	(6.2)	108	(9.8)
1960-70	28,400	(17.8)	211	(19.0)	197	(17.9)
1940-60	55,800	(34.9)	376	(33.8)	365	(33.1)
Before 1940	67,800	(42.4)	455	(41.0)	432	(39.2)
Unit Size						
Efficiency	9,000	(5.6)	286	(9.5)	272	(9.9)
2-3 Rooms	74,000	(46.3)	1,245	(41.4)	1,186	(43.1)
4-5 rooms	60,700	(38.0)	1,168	(38.9)	1,056	(38.4)
6+ rooms	16,100	(10.1)	306	(10.2)	236	(8.6)
Total	159,800		3,005		2,750	

Table B.2   WEIGHTING THE 1987 URBAN INSTITUTE SAMPLE

Income	1981 AHS/(%)		1987 Survey Raw Data/(%)		T-Statistic	Weight
< $15,00	54,400	(38.9)	903	(32.4)	6.98	1.202
$15,000-$25,000	39,300	(28.1)	784	(28.1)	0.00	1.000
$25,000-$35,000	30,400	(21.7)	463	(16.6)	6.49	1.310
$35,000-$50,000	7,400	(5.3)	297	(10.6)	-12.27	0.497
$50,000+	8,300	(5.9)	342	(12.3)	-14.09	0.484

enough to justify reweighting. Table B.2 presents the t-statistics that measure the significance of the differences between the adjusted AHS income distribution and our raw income distribution. In addition, the table shows the weighting factors applied to correct the income distribution. Using these factors, each high-income response in the Urban Institute sample is counted as considerably less than one full household, while each low- and middle-income response is counted as slightly more than one household. All data presented in the body of this report are weighted.

By correcting the income distribution, we expect to achieve a closer match with the AHS distributions of renter households by education, household size, and unit size, as well as a better distribution by ward. The third panel of table B.1 summarizes the weighted survey distribution. The process of weighting by income category had little effect on the other household, dwelling unit, and location distributions. However, the remaining discrepancies are not large enough to warrant a more complex two-way or three-way weighting scheme. Moreover, comparisons of 1974 and 1981 AHS data suggest that D.C. has been experiencing significant shifts in the composition of the renter population, so that the differences between the 1981 AHS and 1987 Urban Institute samples may well reflect population changes rather than sampling errors.

Data Verification

To minimize respondent errors, we attempted to verify three key elements of the household survey by comparing household responses to city records. Specifically, for a subset of 1,319 D.C. respondents who voluntarily supplied their addresses, we obtained data on rent control status, and housing quality from city records. The verification of control status was extremely valuable, and is discussed further in the next section. For rent levels and housing quality, however, we concluded that the city data were less reliable than the household responses. The primary reason for rejecting both the rent and the housing quality measures obtained from city records is that these data apply to properties, while our household survey is made up of individual dwelling unit responses. Thus, city records indicate the ceiling rent for units of a particular size in a property, while the Urban Institute survey provides the actual rent reported by a household for a particular unit. Similarly, city records provide a quality ranking for a whole property, while the Urban Institute survey provides evidence of specific deficiencies reported by a household for a particular unit.

Verification of Tenant Reported Control Status

All survey respondents were asked whether their units were controlled or exempt. For survey respondents who were willing to give their addresses, control status was verified against DCRA registration data. Altogether, control status was verified for 1,103 of the 3,000 households surveyed. As discussed in the body of this report and in Section II of the *Technical Supplement* (volume two of the Institute's rent control report), a large share of D.C. renters did not know their control status. Moreover, for the subsample of verified responses, only 60 percent of tenants had correctly identified their control status. The clear implication of this result is that tenant-reported control status is not a reliable indicator of a unit's actual control status; tenant responses therefore could not be used to distinguish controlled from exempt units for our analysis of the impacts of controls. Therefore, all elements of the analysis in which control status is a factor are limited to the subset of cases for which verified control status was obtained from DCRA records. Tenant responses are used only in our analysis of which groups of tenants are most likely to have accurate information about the control status of their units. Fortunately, the subsample of cases for which control status was verified closely matches the overall sample of D.C. renter households, as shown by table B.3.

FINANCIAL STATEMENTS AND PROVIDER QUESTIONNAIRE

The analysis of ownership and financial characteristics is based on data collected during the fall of 1987 on the financial characteristics of controlled rental properties in the District of Columbia and on the attitudes of D.C. housing providers toward investment in controlled rental housing. In all, the sample of financial statements covered 817 properties, and the housing provider questionnaire was returned for 244 properties. These data have been weighted to represent the distribution of controlled units in the District by the size of the building in which they are located.

Table B.3   CHARACTERISTICS OF THE VERIFIED SUBSAMPLE

	Percentage of Full Sample	Percentage of Verified Subsample
Income:		
< $15,000	32.4	33.8
$15,000-$24,000	28.1	28.7
$25,000-$34,000	16.6	18.3
$35,000-$49,000	10.6	10.3
$50,000+	12.3	9.0
Race:		
Black	59.3	62.5
White	4.1	3.4
Hispanic	5.5	5.0
Other	31.1	29.1
Life-Cycle Group:		
Nonelderly singles	40.7	43.7
Adult groups	14.9	12.7
Elderly	12.2	12.0
Childless couples	11.0	9.6
Husband-wife families	8.5	9.1
Female-headed families	12.8	12.9

Sample Design

Table B.4 presents the number of rental properties and rental units by building size for the District of Columbia as a whole, based on a listing of these properties and their characteristics maintained in the District's Metropolitan Area Geographic Information System (MAGIS). This universe includes controlled and exempt properties, but excludes condominium

Table B.4   CONTROLLED RENTAL PROPERTIES: SAMPLE
             CHARACTERISTICS

| Building | Actual | | Sample | |
Size (Units)	Buildings	Units	Buildings	Units
1-2	26,828	30,320	19	23
3-4	4,188	15,455	18	68
5-9	1,277	8,367	152	1,023
10-19	1,499	21,735	128	1,789
20-49	788	24,285	100	3,172
50-99	217	15,325	31	2,269
100-199	94	14,053	51	6,721
200+	69	22,774	33	11,777
Total	34,960	152,314	532	26,842

and cooperative buildings in which some or all units are
rented. A separate list of rental units in condo and co-op
projects was also developed, as explained further below.

Lawrence Johnson and Associates, a subcontractor to The
Urban Institute, designed the sampling methodology for
selecting a stratified random sample of 1,900 addresses from
the MAGIS list of D.C. rental properties. Properties with
fewer than five units were overrepresented in this sample
because most of these properties were expected to be exempt
from controls, and very large properties were oversampled
because they account for such a significant share of the rental
housing stock as a whole.

In addition, a random sample of 100 rental units in
condominium and 50 cooperative buildings was also selected
from the MAGIS data files. This sample was not stratified by
building size, but simply provided a random selection of
rental condo and co-op units.

Financial Data Collection

For the 1,900 sampled rental properties and the 150 condo and co-op addresses, Urban Institute and LJA staff examined registration data maintained by the DCRA. For all cases in which a registration file could be found, the 1985 registration statement was reproduced, indicating control status, reasons for exemptions from rent control and--for controlled properties--a 1985 financial statement. Registration files were found for 1,375 of the properties in our sample, and financial statements were obtained for 817 controlled properties. File data on the 150 rental condo and co-op units were less complete, probably because a large share of these units are not subject to controls, and because they change from renter- to owner-occupancy with relative frequency. These data were not coded and computerized, owing to their incompleteness and ambiguity.

The financial data for the 817 controlled properties with 1985 registration form were coded and computerized by LJA staff. These data were then carefully reviewed by Urban Institute staff, and three types of errors were systematically corrected. First, some of the registration forms had been filled out incompletely or incorrectly by the housing providers. These errors were corrected by examining the form as a whole, and in a few cases, by calling the housing provider to verify essential information. Second, some of the forms were incorrectly coded or key-punched. And, finally, some of the registration forms applied to multiple addresses, which are apparently treated as combined "rental projects" for accounting purposes. In cases where we could not determine the number of units to which a registration form applied, financial data had to be dropped from our sample. Altogether, a total of 194 cases had to be dropped, and 91 cases were combined into projects consisting of multiple buildings. The final dataset consists of complete financial statements for 532 controlled rental properties--consisting of 26,842 units.

Because we sampled at different rates based on the size of rental properties, and because financial data were not available for all of the properties in the sample, we have calculated weights for all of the rental properties in our sample to reflect their probability of being selected. As shown in table B.5, property weights were assigned to each building size class to reflect the actual distribution of controlled properties by building size. Thus, each property's weight is the reciprocal of its probability of being selected from all controlled properties.

In our analysis, all data are reported on a weighted per-unit basis. Thus, financial and other characteristics are adjusted for the number of units in the property and are weighted to reflect both the property's contribution to the controlled D.C. housing stock and its probability of being in our sample. This means that our analysis and results focus on the average controlled unit or the distribution of controlled units, rather than on buildings--which contribute varying numbers of housing units to the stock.

Provider Questionnaire

To supplement the data gathered from DCRA registration forms, questionnaires were mailed (in November 1987) to the owners and/or managers of all the controlled rental properties for which financial data were available. These questionnaires were designed to gather additional information about ownership form; size of holdings; reasons for investment in D.C. rental property; attitudes toward the rental market, and regulatory environment, and the D.C. Tenant Assistance Program (TAP); and plans for future rental housing investment. Because of the length of the questionnaire and its importance to our analysis, an aggressive follow-

Table B.5   CONTROLLED RENTAL PROPERTIES: SAMPLE
WEIGHTS

Building Size (Units)	Share Units Controlled	Estimated Number Controlled Units	Sample Weight
1-2	0.46	14,038	610.35
3-4	0.46	7,126	104.80
5-9	0.75	6,275	6.13
10-19	0.86	18,770	10.49
20-49	0.91	22,109	6.97
50-99	0.90	13,846	6.10
100-199	0.81	11,317	1.68
200+	0.82	18,634	1.58

Note: The share of units in each building size category was obtained
from our survey of renter households (see "Technical Memorandum
#1," March 1988). The estimated number of controlled units in each
size category was obtained by multiplying the share that is
controlled by the total number of units from table b.1. The sample
weight for each size category was obtained by dividing the total
number of controlled units by the total number of sample units.

up effort was pursued to maximize the number of completed
forms. Specifically, all survey recipients were called within
two weeks of the date when questionnaires were mailed, and
to ensure that survey forms had been received and were
being completed; staff responsible for these call-backs were
well informed about the study and the role of the provider
survey in the study design, and were trained to answer
questions and respond to concerns about the questionnaire;
all of the providers who owned and/or managed more than
15 of our sample properties were contacted directly by Urban
Institute research staff, who stressed the importance of
providers' responses to the objectives of the study as a whole
and offered assistance in the completion of the questionnaires;

altogether, survey recipients received at least three call-backs if they did not return their questionnaires within a six-week response period; in addition, intensive assistance in completing the question-naires was provided to respondents with particularly large numbers of sample properties.

This follow-up strategy was effective in generating completed questionnaires for a total of 244 controlled properties, accounting for 12,801 units. In other words, supplemental property descriptions and attitudinal data were obtained for 46 percent of the properties and 48 percent of the units in our sample. Moreover, as shown in table B.6, the properties for which surveys were returned are comparable--with respect to size and inspection rating--to the sample as a whole. In other words, no obvious classes of controlled rental properties were underrepresented in the provider survey.

COMPONENTS OF INVENTORY CHANGE

This section outlines local records used to inventory additions to and losses from the District's rental housing stock from May 1985 through April 1987. These data were assembled in the fall of 1987.

Sources and Handling of Inventory Additions Data

Additions data were culled from Certificate of Occupancy records kept by the DCRA for May 1, 1985 to April 30, 1987. Certificates of Occupancy were chosen as the preferred source of inventory additions data because:

1. They best reflect the date that a unit is ready to come on the market;

Table B.6   PROVIDER SURVEY RESPONDENTS

| Building | Sample Properties | | Survey Respondents | |
Size (Units)	Number	%	Number	%
1-2	19	3.6	2	.8
3-4	18	3.4	12	5
5-9	152	28.6	72	30
10-19	128	24.1	61	25.4
20-49	100	18.8	37	15.4
50-99	31	5.8	13	5.4
100-199	51	9.6	26	10.8
200+	33	6.2	27	7.1

2. They more selectively record actual additions, in contrast to typical building permit data that document units authorized or planned but not always completed; and,

3. They provided a rich amount of property information in a form that was useful and relatively accessible for our study purposes.

Records on a rental property's present and previous use, present and previous number of units, and reason for obtaining a Certificate of Occupancy provided the basis for categorizing each addition by component in our inventory change model. We verified the larger additions and clarified any ambiguous records by telephone with the owner or agent listed on the Certificate of Occupancy. Several records were consolidated into one, in cases where the additions or buildings could be determined to be part of a single project.

The figures on the number of additions will slightly undercount (rather than overcount) the actual number that occurred, because of the nature of the data source and because we conservatively counted only verified additions. Specifically:

1. Only those who filed for a Certificate of Occupancy were included in the data (although all are required to do so, some activity always goes on outside official records);

2. Roughly 15 days of the daily Certificate issuance log (our entry to the actual permit files) were unavailable;

3. Several possible small inventory changes were left unclarified (and therefore excluded) because of the difficulty involved in checking them (owner could not be reached, etc.). Intensive effort was made to check the larger changes, and many of the remaining ambiguous records are believed to involve ownership change only;

4. A conservative assumption was made about single-family dwellings converting to two-unit flats: where the prior tenure of the single-family dwelling was unknown, it was assumed that only one rental unit was added to the inventory, even though the owner may have moved (thus actually adding two rental units).

A best guess correction, taking into account all of the preceding factors except activity outside legal channels, might add only another 125 units, or less than 5 percent.

Sources and Handling of Inventory Losses Data

All units leaving the rental inventory are required to go through the evictions office at DCRA, even where the tenant has already vacated the unit. Section 501 of the Rental Housing Act of 1985 governs these removals. We collected data from the required filings with DCRA and the Notices to Vacate where the reason given was one of the following:

- 501(d)--"to recover possession of the rental unit for the person's immediate and personal use and occupancy as a dwelling";

- 501(e)--"to sell the rental unit . . . for the immediate personal use and occupancy by another person";

- 501(g)--"for the purpose of immediately demolishing the housing accommodation in which the rental unit is located";

- 501(i)--"for the immediate purpose of discontinuing the housing use and occupancy of the rental unit."

Restrictions, too detailed to cover here, accompany each provision. Additional required information provided the basis for assigning each loss to a component in our inventory change model. Housing providers are also required to indicate their registration and/or exemption status under rent control. Information on mergers, which require structural alterations and recertification, came from Certificates of Occupancy.

Again, the count of losses is unlikely to be exact. While most instances of noncompliance would involve evictions or notices to vacate where the tenant was somehow undesirable to the housing provider and the unit was subsequently rerented, an undetermined number of actual losses from the inventory take place outside of District records, and would be difficult if not impossible to document. On the other hand, we are aware of at least one instance where a properly-filed notice to vacate did not lead to a loss from the inventory, because the owner's reasons for removing the units were negated by a voluntary rent increase negotiated with tenants.

Sources and Handling of Condominium Registration Data

Separate data were collected on the condominiums newly registered with DCRA. We were able to study this limited number of properties extensively, tracing each from registration log, to application log, to the D.C. Municipal Automated Geographic Information System (MAGIS) and the private LUSK directories. This process allowed us to determine as nearly as possible the percentage of each property's units that are rented and the appropriate component of inventory change involved. Registrations involving new construction, conversion of nonrental properties, or rehabilitation of vacant properties may add units to the city's rental inventory, whereas those involving the conversion of apartment units may remove some units from the rental inventory. Since condominiums are legal entities involving the form in which title is held, condominium registration data should be complete. Conversion and sale are not possible without being registered. MAGIS's determination of the tenure status of each unit is based on whether or not the address to which the assessment and property tax bill are mailed corresponds to the property address.

To determine whether these condominium-associated components of change should supplement our Certificate of

Occupancy and evictions data, the amount the sources overlap, and to what extent the date ranges are comparable, we cross-checked the data sources. Those additions that were not already listed or that were found to have Certificates of Occupancy outside of the relevant date range were discarded, and the remainder added to the additions file. Loss data were similarly supplemented. In all, condominium records added about 10 percent to both the addition and loss files.

Geographic Analysis

To take full advantage of the detailed property information gathered from our intensive data collection effort from District records, The Urban Institute contracted with the Computer Mapping and Spatial Analysis (CMSA) Laboratory at the University of Maryland. The addresses of properties where additions and losses occurred were digitized, linked with other data about each property, and overlaid onto District ward boundaries using the CMSA Laboratory's sophisticated geographic information system, ARCINFO.

Digitizing the property addresses of rental additions and losses allowed visual analysis of the geographic distribution of stock change activity in the District by component and size. It also enabled us to produce rental inventory change statistics by ward, important information that would otherwise not have been available.

Except for tenure change from rental to owner-occupied, all sites where rental units were either added or lost were digitized. Instances of tenure change, although not representing an overwhelming number of units, contained more sites than the other 10 components combined. Thus, a 25 percent sample of these sites was deemed more than sufficient to establish the geographic distribution of this activity. (See Section III of the *Technical Supplement* for complete results of the mapping analysis.)

Telephone Interview Procedure

Components of inventory change accounting for more than 15 percent of additions or losses were deemed worthy of more detailed study. Survey instruments guided the in-depth interviews with housing providers. Of particular interest were the motivations of housing providers' supply decisions, their opinions of rent control and the regulatory environment, subsidy programs, and building and tenant characteristics. Project resources, the small size of some of the components, and the difficulty of contacting owners limited the number of surveys for each component and dictated the largely reportorial--as opposed to statistical--tone of the discussion of survey results.

Between the three main components of additions surveyed, 17 interviews were conducted with housing providers who were together responsible for 25 percent of all additions to the D.C. rental inventory between May 1985 and April 1987. Interviews with four owners responsible for new construction covered 10 percent of the newly constructed units; the remaining owners could not be contacted or would not participate. Interviews with seven owners responsible for the rehabilitation of nonresidential structures covered 42 percent of these units. Interviews with six owners responsible for the rehabilitation of vacant structures covered 39 percent of these units. Differences between components were not significant enough to remark on in the text of this report, given the small sample.

Between the two main components of losses surveyed, 11 interviews were conducted with housing providers who were together responsible for 6 percent of all losses to the D.C. rental inventory between May 1985 and April 1987. Interviews with four owners responsible for retrievable losses covered 24 percent of these units. Interviews with seven owners responsible for tenure change losses covered 3 percent of these losses; the similarities of these seven small owners made further interviewing unnecessary. The significant differences between the responses of owners in each of the two components are noted in the text.

PRO FORMA FINANCIAL ANALYSIS

Property Appreciation

Property appreciation is an essential element of profit to investors in rental real estate. Each year, the cash returns realized by an investor are essentially supplemented by the increase in property value. However, appreciation gains can only be realized by selling or refinancing the property, which obviously does not happen every year. Therefore, many measures of return to investment in rental real estate discount appreciation benefits, to reflect the fact that they will not be realized until sometime in the future. For this analysis we have adopted a simpler approach. Since we have no data on how frequently D.C. rental properties are sold or refinanced, and since our primary interest is in comparing the profitability of different classes of rental real estate, we have not discounted the value of appreciation gains. Instead, using data on average assessed property values in 1982 and 1987, we have estimated an average annual appreciation rate for each building size category. These annual rates are then applied to average per-unit property values for different types of controlled rental units to yield an annual estimate of the dollar value of appreciation gains. Table C.1 presents average assessed property values for 1982 and 1987, obtained from the District's Metropolitan Area Geographic Information System (MAGIS). These values have been used to estimate an

Table C.1   AVERAGE ASSESSED VALUE BY BUILDING SIZE: 1982, 1987

Building Size (Units)	Average Assessed Value ($)		Average Annual Percent Change
	1982	1987	
1-2	85,120	103,722	4.03
3-4	66,072	97,071	8.00
5-9	101,832	133,057	5.49
10-19	140,670	172,827	4.20
20-49	355,656	445,486	4.61
50-99	1,100,507	1,357,675	4.29
100-249	3,290,420	3,641,775	2.05
250+	8,778,525	8,306,554	-0.01

average annual rate of property appreciation for each building size category.

Federal Tax Benefits

Until 1986, the differential tax treatment of competing investment opportunities often played a central role in shaping investor decisions. Housing, in particular, has been the beneficiary of at least two decades of preferential tax treatment. The two primary tax benefits available to investors in rental housing were accelerated depreciation and a reduced tax rate on long-term capital gains. We have applied a set of fairly conservative assumptions about the tax treatment applicable prior to 1986 to approximate the after-tax return on investment in different types of D.C. rental properties. As discussed earlier, the goal of these assumptions is to allow us to compare different classes of property under different economic and regulatory assumptions, not to produce definitive measures of provider profits. The after-tax return on equity has been calculated as:

Return = (Income - Expenditures + Appreciation - Taxes)/Equity,

where

> *Income* = total actual income per unit;
>
> *Expenditures* = total operating expenditures
>
> *Appreciation* = average annual rate of appreciation times per-unit value;

Taxes = t(Income - Expenditures - Depreciation) + c(Appreciation).

> t = marginal rate--tested at both 35 percent and 50 percent;
>
> > *Depreciation* = (1/15) Depreciable basis;
> >
> > *Depreciable basis* = 85% x Value;
>
> c = capital gains tax rate--half the marginal tax rate.

On the next page table C.2 presents appreciation and tax calculations for several key types of controlled rental units.

Table C.2   CALCULATING AFTER-TAX RETURN ON EQUITY

| | For the Average Controlled Unit in a Building with: | |
	1-2 Units	3-4 Units
Net Income	-$181	$110
Equity	$33,394	$10,981
Income/Equity	-0.54%	1.00%
Appreciation Rate	4.03%	8.00%
Appreciation (income + appreciation)/equity	$2,441 6.77%	$1,805 17.44%
After-tax income (@ 50%)	$3,455	$2,048
After-tax income (@ 35%)	$3,097	$2,008
After-tax return (@ 50%)	10.35%	18.65%
After-tax return (@ 35%)	9.27%	18.28%

| | For the Average Controlled Unit in a Building with: | |
	20-49 Units	100-249 Units
Net Income	$578	$1,153
Equity	$10,370	$10,668
Income/Equity	5.57	10.81
Appreciation Rate	4.61%	2.05%
Appreciation (income + appreciation)/equity	$567 11.04%	$349 14.08%
After tax income (@ 50%)	$1,063	$1,320
After tax income (@ 35%)	$1,088	$1,374
After tax return (@ 50%)	10.25%	12.37%
After tax return (@ 35%)	10.49%	12.88%

MARKET RENT ESTIMATION

This section details the methodology used for estimating what D.C. rents would be in the absence of controls. The methodology consists of four basic steps:

1. Estimating the relationship between housing unit attributes and rent levels in 1974--before the imposition of rent control in the District of Columbia;

2. Using this relationship to estimate what units now available for rent in D.C. would have rented for in 1974;

3. Increasing these precontrol rent estimates to reflect the rate of rent inflation typical of uncontrolled central cities between 1974 and 1987; and

4. Adjusting these final market rent estimates to reflect for locational rent differences that prevail today.

Housing Unit Attributes and Rents--1974

The methodology we adopted assumes that the relative value or cost of different types of rental units would have remained reasonably constant over the 1974-87 period, had it not been for the imposition of rent control. In other words, the proportionate effect of an extra bedroom or a better quality unit on rent would have remained the same, even though overall rent levels would certainly have increased. Therefore, our first step was to estimate the relationships that prevailed before 1974 between housing unit attributes and unit rents in the District of Columbia.

Table D.1 presents the results of a multivariate regression equation expressing gross rent as a function of unit attributes.[1] The estimated regression coefficients in this equation can be interpreted as the "prices" of the various attributes. The objective of a regression equation of this kind is to explain as much of the observed variation in rents as possible, so that the equation can be used for predictive purposes. Therefore, we experimented with several alternative specifications, and the equation presented in table D.1 represents the one with the greatest explanatory power and the most significant coefficients.

1974 Rents for 1987 Rental Units

The next step was to use the equation outlined in table D.1 to estimate what the units that are available in D.C. today would have rented for in 1974. To predict a unit's 1974 rent, its attributes--values for all of the explanatory variables in the regression--were "plugged into" the regression equation. In other words, the value of each attribute was multiplied by the corresponding coefficient, and the results were summed to arrive at a predicted rent. This technique was used to estimate 1974 rents for all of the units in our 1987 sample of D.C. households.

These 1974 rent estimates can be used in two ways. First, they provide the basis for our estimates of 1987 rents in the absence of controls for the 1974 and 1987 period. More

Table D.1   1974 GROSS RENT REGRESSION EQUATION: D.C.
             UNITS

Attributes	Coefficient	Standard Error
Intercept	6.027[a]	.040
Single-family house	-.151[a]	.018
Duplex	-.318[a]	.024
3- to 4-unit building	-.337[a]	.017
5- to 9-unit building	-.268[a]	.016
10- to 19-unit building	-.206[a]	.014
20- to 49-unit building	-.194[a]	.018
Efficiency	-.609[a]	.030
2-room unit	-.484[a]	.026
3-room unit	-.306[a]	.021
4-room unit	-.198[a]	.024
5-room unit	-.081[a]	.020
No complete bathroom	-.528[a]	.031
1 bathroom	-.263[a]	.030
Central city	-.023	.012
Recent mover	.020	.019
Moved in 1-2 years ago	.122[a]	.012
Moved in 2-3 years ago	.079[a]	.013
Moved in 3-4 years ago	.050[a]	.015
Moved in 4-5 years ago	.069[a]	.023
Household head is black	-1.22[a]	.023
Household head is white	.090[a]	.023
R^2	49.49	

Source: 1987 Urban Institute "Tenant Survey."

Note: The dependent variable is the natural logarithm of gross rent.

a. Significance at the 99 percent confidence level

specifically, the ratio of a unit's 1987 rent to our estimate of what the same unit would have rented for in 1974 reflects rent inflation, controlling for any changes in unit quality. We compared constant quality rent inflation indexes for D.C. and the surrounding suburbs to the rate of inflation in median rents, and found virtually no difference. This reassured us that the change in median rent levels is a reasonable approximation of a constant quality rent inflation index for other central cities.

Inflating 1974 Rents to 1987

The third step in our methodology was to inflate the 1974 rents for 1987 units upward to reflect the average rate of rent inflation that would have prevailed in D.C. in the absence of controls. As discussed in the body of this report, examination of rent trends in the Washington, D.C., suburbs and in other central cities in the Northeast and Middle-Atlantic regions suggests that rents in D.C. would have increased by about 9.5 percent per year on average in the absence of rent control. The estimated 1974 rents for all 1987 D.C. units were inflated at this rate to yield 1987 estimates of rents in the absence of controls.

Adjusting for Location Differences

Finally, we adjusted the 1987 market rent estimates for variations in rents among D.C. wards. More specifically, neighborhood conditions clearly play a role in determining rent levels; two otherwise comparable units located in different surroundings may well have very different rent levels. Our 1974 regression equation does not include a location variable, because none was available in the AHS data. However, ward identifiers are available for a large share of the D.C. units in our 1987 sample. We concluded that

Table D.2   RENT ADJUSTMENT FACTORS, BY D.C. WARD

Ward	Adjustment Factor	Ward	Adjustment Factor
1	0.9392	5	0.9197
2	1.0541	6	1.0391
3	1.0656	7	0.9658
4	1.0621	8	0.9357

Source: Urban Institute calculations.

the relative rents of housing units in different wards--after controlling for unit size, quality, and length of tenure--are probably about the same today as they would be in the absence of controls. In other words, there is no reason to believe that rent control has affected ward rent differentials. Therefore, we estimated the relative price of a comparable housing unit located in each of the District's eight wards. These price adjustment factors, presented in table D.2, were based on the coefficients for location variables in a gross rent regression estimated for D.C. rental units in 1987. These factors were applied to the estimates of 1987 market rents obtained from the 1974 gross rent regression. Specifically, the estimated market rent of each 1987 unit was adjusted upward or downward to reflect the relative advantages or disadvantages of the ward in which it is located.

Note, appendix D

1. Actually, the dependent variable in our regression equations is the natural log of gross rent. This means that the coefficients reflect the percent change in rent attributable to a unit change in any of the various explanatory variables.

Appendix E

PROFITS IN THE ABSENCE OF CONTROLS

Impacts of Rent Control

To estimate the impacts of controls in returns to rental property investment, we simulated the effects of market rent levels on pro forma financial statements of properties in different size categories. The first step was to convert our market rent estimates into rent revenue estimates for controlled providers. The market rents estimated using the hedonic methodology outlined earlier are $95-$100 higher on average than actual gross rents. However, after limiting the sample to controlled units, and subtracting utilities paid directly by tenants, we found that contract rents for controlled properties would average about 33 percent higher in the absence of controls. This average applied consistently gross building size categories. Therefore, we applied a 33 percent increase to gross rent revenues to the average pro forma financial statement for each building size.

Higher rent revenues produce a second key change in a property's financial statement--higher property value. We retained the existing rent-to-value ratios for each property size category in order to obtain estimates of property values in the absence of controls. When property values increase, property taxes, interest costs, equity, and appreciation benefits also rise. Again, we retained the existing relationships between property taxes and value, debt and value, interest costs and debt, and rate of appreciation. Results are presented in table E.1.

Table E.1   CALCULATING AFTER-TAX RETURNS IN THE ABSENCE OF RENT CONTROL

	For the Average Controlled Unit in a Building with:							
	1-2 Units		3-4 Units		20-49 Units		100-249 Units	
	Actual	Market	Actual	Market	Actual	Market	Actual	Market
Revenues	$4,573	$6,082	$3,053	$4,060	$4,179	$5,558	$4,811	$6,399
Value	$60,534	$80,510	$22,564	$30,010	$12,308	$16,370	$17,010	$22,623
Equity	$33,394	$44,414	$10,981	$14,605	$10,370	$13,792	$10,668	$14,188
Property Taxes	$692	$920	$273	$363	$201	$267	$239	$318
Interest	$1,416	$1,883	$1,003	$1,334	$384	$511	$480	$638
Appreciation	$2,441	$3,246	$1,805	$2,400	$567	$754	$349	$464
Total Expenditures	$4,754	$5,766	$1,805	$2,400	$3,601	$4,676	$3,658	$5,147
Net Income	-$181	$316	$110	$348	$578	$882	$1,153	$1,252
Income/equity	-0.54%	0.71%	1.00%	2.39%	5.57%	6.40%	10.81%	8.82%
(income and appreciation)/ equity	6.77%	8.02%	17.44%	18.82%	11.04%	11.86%	14.08%	12.09%
After-tax return	10.35%	10.97%	18.65%	19.34%	10.25%	10.66%	12.37%	11.38%

Tax Reform Act (TRA) of 1986

The impacts on investment returns of TRA 1986 are extremely complex and sensitive to the circumstances of individual investors. However, two key features of the recent tax reform have been incorporated into our pro forma financial statements--restricted depreciation schedules and reduced tax rates. As shown in table E.2, we modified our basic calculations of after-tax return on equity to reflect much slower depreciation schedules and lower marginal tax rates.

Table E.2   CALCULATING AFTER-TAX RETURN ON EQUITY SUBJECT TO TAX REFORM ACT OF 1986

| | For the Average Controlled Unit in a Building with: | | | |
	1-2 Units	3-4 Units	20-49 Units	100-249 Units
Net income	-$181	$110	$578	$1,153
Equity	$33,394	$10,981	$10,370	$10,668
Income/equity	-0.54%	1.00%	5.57%	10.81%
Appreciation Rate	4.03%	8.00%	4.61%	2.05%
Appreciation (income and appreciation)/ equity	6.77%	17.44%	11.04%	14.08%
After-tax income (@ 35%)	$2,124	$1,596	$946	$1,247
After-tax return (@ 35%)	6.36%	14.53%	9.12%	11.69%

OPERATING COST INFLATION

The rental increase of "general applicability," or automatic increase, is linked to changes in the consumer price index for urban wage earners and clerical workers. Operating costs, however, may depart from general price trends. Therefore, the automatic rent increases may over- or undercompensate for real changes in operating costs. Moreover, given the different operating cost profiles of buildings of varying size, some property types may be relatively disadvantaged under this adjustment mechanism. This analysis estimates the change in operating costs for rental properties according to building size classification.

To estimate changes in operating costs for rental properties of different size classifications, we estimated the general price changes for each operating cost item between 1981 and 1987, then weighted these data by their shares of operating costs for properties in our eight building size categories.

Operating Cost Components

We did not attempt to price each component of operating costs, choosing, rather, to focus on those items comprising the bulk of total operating expenses. Neither did we fully price each component according to actual usage--on a per-job basis, for example, in plumbing repair--but relied on general price trends for labor or other standard costs units.

Service and Maintenance Costs

On the advice of a housing provider representative on the D.C. Rent Control Advisory Committee and a representative of the Property Managers Association, we consulted several large contractors in each category of maintenance typically performed on rental property to obtain changes in skilled labor rates for each type of job. As labor rates represent the bulk of the cost of each maintenance activity, changes in labor costs should accurately reflect changes in overall per-job costs. Maintenance categories included:

- Painting/decorating
- Plumbing
- Heating/ventilating/air-conditioning (HVAC)
- Elevator repair and maintenance
- Roofing
- Groundskeeping

For all categories except groundskeeping, we collected data on changes in hourly rates from one or two large contractors. Groundskeeping labor costs are assumed to track the minimum wage.

To each hourly rate, we added an estimated cost for Work-men's Compensation insurance, Supplemental Security Income (Social Security), and Unemployment Insurance. Workmen's Compensation was valued at the midpoint of the range of rates provided by a major carrier, and was costed in an amount equal to the hourly wage. Unemployment Insurance was assumed to be the average for the District as reported by the District Office of Employment Security. Social Security was applied at the statutory rate.

Table F.1   ESTIMATED HOURLY LABOR RATES BY
             MAINTENANCE CATEGORY: 1981, 1987

	1981 Rate ($)	1987 Rate ($)	Percent Change
Plumbing	38.90	45.40	+16.7
HVAC	40.00	51.00	27.5
Elevator	57.20	73.70	28.8
Roofing	34.30	43.10	25.7
Electrical	32.00	40.80	27.5
Painting	22.90	28.40	24.0
Grounds	3.20	4.30	34.4
Average	32.64	40.96	25.5

Table F.1 shows the estimated hourly rates and total rate change percentages for each maintenance category. The percentage increases across categories show remarkable uniformity.

Utility Cost

Utility cost data were estimated using the consumer price index for this component for the Washington, D.C., standard metropolitan statistical area (SMSA). From January 1981 through December 1987, the fuel and other utilities index increased 30 percent.

Insurance

Insurance costs vary with the rate charged and the amount of required coverage. Rates vary with the type of property be-

Table F.2   PROPERTY INSURANCE RATES BY BUILDING
             TYPE (per $100 coverage)

| | Joisted Masonry | | Percent |
	1981 Fire	1987 Fire	Change
Building:			
Up to 10	.297	.330	+11.1
11 to 30	.396	.437	10.3
Over 30	.51	.56	9.8
Contents:			
Up to 10	.297	.330	+11.1
11 to 30	.341	.378	10.9
Over 30	.374	.414	10.7

Source: ISO Commercial Risk Services, 1983 and 1987, <u>Coverage Lines Manual</u>. 1983 rates unchanged from 1981.

Note: Joisted Masonry was selected because it represents the upper bound in the percent change in rates. Rate increases for other construction classes --frame, non-combustible, masonry noncombustible, and modified fire resistive--have been slightly lower.

ing insured and are dependent on factors such as building size, age and condition of the structure, quality of original construction, presence of an elevator, any special fire pre-vention features, and location. Of course, the range of property types in the District is wide. However, for purposes of comparison, unique building characteristics were ignored. Only building size rate differentials were considered. Fire insurance rates by building size are presented in table F.2. Given the consistency in the direction of rate change, we can

Table F.3   ESTIMATED CHANGES IN INSURANCE COSTS
BY BUILDING SIZE, 1981-87

Size Category (Units)	Percent Change
1-2	+35.4
3-4	94.3
5-9	41.5
10-19	38.2
20-49	40.1
50-99	32.7
100-249	36.2
250+	25.9

apply the average changes for these property categories more generally to other types of rental property.

In addition to the change in rates, the amounts of required coverage differ as well. For fire insurance coverage, we assumed that coverage changes are directly proportionate to changes in assessed property value. For different categories of building size, we computed the change in median assessed value form 1981 to 1986 as supplied by the District's Planning Office, and extrapolated the trend to cover the additional year. We then used these percent changes, together with the changes in rates, to produce a total estimated change in insurance costs by building size. These are shown in table F.3.

Property Taxes and Other Cost Items

Property tax rates did not change over the period. The percent change in property taxes is the same as the change in median assessment for each size category. Table F.4 shows the change in median assessment for each building size cate-

Table F.4   CHANGE IN MEDIAN ASSESSED
             VALUATION BY BUILDING SIZE
             CATEGORY, 1982-87

Units in Structure	Percent Change
1-2	22.0
3-4	75.0
5-9	27.5
10-19	24.5
20-49	26.8
50-99	20.3
100-249	23.5
250+	14.1

gory. Other principal operating costs items include manage-
ment fees--assumed to remain constant over the period--and
administrative costs, including legal fees, telephone, and
advertising. We did not attempt to price the cost changes of
these latter items.

Operating Cost Shares

The estimated cost changes for each component of operating
costs must be weighted by their relative shares of total
operating costs for each building size. These weights are
presented in table F.5. With the exception of single- and two-
unit properties, cost ratios are roughly similar across building
size categories for most expenditure items. One- and two-
unit buildings typically contain individually metered rental
units, accounting for the low share of operating expenses
attributable to utility cost for the building type. Conversely,
fees and insurance, and property taxes, comprise a higher

Table F.5   OPERATING COST COMPONENTS AS A PERCENTAGE OF
TOTAL OPERATING COSTS BY BUILDING SIZE

| | Building Size (units) | | | | | | | |
	1-2 (%)	3-4 (%)	5-9 (%)	10-19 (%)	20-49 (%)	50-100 (%)	101-250 (%)	250+ (%)
Service and Maintenance	22	24	25	23	21	20	17	18
Administrative	16	9	7	8	9	7	9	12
Utilities	9	32	34	41	38	40	36	34
Operating	11	9	10	10	16	16	19	19
Fees and insurance	19	7	7	5	8	4	7	7
Property taxes	21	14	12	8	6	8	8	6
Management fees	3	5	7	6	5	5	4	4

Source: Urban Institute calculations based on 1985 D.C. Registrations data.

share of total operating expenses, reflecting high per-unit assessed values.

Rental Property Total Operating Cost Increases

For properties in each size category, the increase in each cost item is weighted by the percentage of total operating costs represented by that item. A weighted average is then computed. On the following page table F.6 shows the resulting estimated operating cost increase for each building size.

Table F.6   ESTIMATED OPERATING
             EXPENSE INCREASE BY BUILDING
             SIZE, 1981-87

Building Size (Units)	Percent Increase
1-2	31
3-4	41
5-9	33
10-19	31
20-49	35
50-99	30
100-249	30
250+	29
Automatic Rent Increase	31